The
EVERYTHING®
Slow Cooking
for a Crowd
Cookbook

Dear Reader:

My life is unbelievably busy. I bet yours is, too. I could simplify my life, but then I'd miss out on so much I enjoy—like fixing up my old farmhouse, reading, and spending time with my family. Sound familiar?

I have two main strategies, however, that help keep me sane. First, I try to be organized. I make lists and plan ahead whenever possible. Second, I always try to be efficient. This is the big one. Why make three or four small trips to the store, when I can prepare a comprehensive list to get everything the first time? Why buy one loaf of bread, when I can buy five and freeze four?

A slow cooker is designed to be efficient; that's why I use it. It doesn't need babysitting and is very forgiving. I always double or triple recipes and freeze the extra, whether I'm cooking for myself or for a group. If I didn't use my slow cooker, I wouldn't have time to read that new novel, fix that barn door, or have a party!

I hope this book helps you get the most out of your slow cooker—and your life. Best of luck!

Katie Thompson

The EVERYTHING Series

Editorial

Publishing Director	Gary M. Krebs
Associate Managing Editor	Laura M. Daly
Associate Copy Chief	Brett Palana-Shanahan
Acquisitions Editor	Kate Burgo
Development Editor	Katie McDonough
Associate Production Editor	Casey Ebert

Production

Director of Manufacturing	Susan Beale
Associate Director of Production	Michelle Roy Kelly
Cover Design	Paul Beatrice
	Erick DaCosta
	Matt LeBlanc
Design and Layout	Colleen Cunningham
	Holly Curtis
	Erin Dawson
	Sorae Lee
Series Cover Artist	Barry Littmann

THE

EVERYTHING®

SLOW COOKING
FOR A CROWD
COOKBOOK

Features 300 appetizing
home-cooked recipes

Katie Thompson

Adams Media
Avon, Massachusetts

This book is dedicated to my mother, who believes in me.

An Everything® Series Book.
Everything® and everything.com® are registered trademarks of F+W Publications, Inc.

Published by Adams Media, an F+W Publications Company
57 Littlefield Street, Avon, MA 02322. U.S.A.
www.adamsmedia.com

ISBN: 1-59337-391-0
Printed in the United States of America.

J I H G F E D C B A

Library of Congress Cataloging-in-Publication Data
Thompson, Katie, 1962-
The everything slow cooking for a crowd cookbook :
features 300 appetizing home-cooked recipes / Katie Thompson.
p. cm. -- (An everything series book)
Includes bibliographical references and index.
ISBN 1-59337-391-0 (alk. paper)
1. Electric cookery, Slow. 2. Quantity cookery. I. Title. II. Series: Everything series.

TX827.T44 2005
641.5'7--dc22
2005018841

This book is available at quantity discounts for bulk purchases.
For information, please call 1-800-872-5627.

contents

acknowledgments

Thank you to my friends
who helped with this project and more.

introduction

So you're going to entertain? Excellent! But you've got lots to do. There are menus to make, foods to prepare, and drinks to mix. The list of preparations seems endless. You may be wondering how you're going to get everything done with a limited amount of time.

Believe it or not, one of the most efficient ways to entertain is to go slowly. Slowly? Yes—you can use your time more effectively if you harness the power of your slow cooker. In fact, you can go even slower. Borrow or buy another slow cooker—or two or four—and your job will be even easier.

You may think this sounds crazy. Everyone in today's world seems to be searching for a way to do things faster. There is high-speed Internet, one-touch speed-dial, instant messaging, and the popular power nap. There's even fast food, speed dating, and express checkout at the grocery store. But slower is better in this case because your slow cooker helps you multitask. Multitasking means efficiency. A slow cooker will do the work of an oven, a stovetop, and a serving dish, all while you take care of other things. On the morning of your party, you can set up one slow cooker with an appetizer, another with hot sandwiches, and a third with a dessert. And of course, you'll need a couple more to prepare steaming, aromatic drinks for your guests.

Once the ingredients are in the slow cooker, you are free. Slow cookers keep an eye on themselves, don't need stirring, don't mind if you're late, and can do their job wherever you can run an extension cord. When guests arrive, the slow cookers are already in position. Just set out the plates and silverware, open the lids, and let your guests enjoy your creations.

A slow cooker can help you look like a pro, even if you rarely cook or bake from scratch. And if you're already experienced in the kitchen and don't think you need another appliance, take a moment to reconsider. Slow cooking isn't cheating—it's just smart!

Entertaining is the best opportunity to use slow cookers. Using slow cookers for a party allows you to prepare dishes hours or even days ahead of time, serve multiple hot dishes at once, and keep food and drinks warm for the duration of your party—all without the use of your oven or stovetop.

Whether your event is a rowdy Super Bowl party, a child's birthday celebration, or a small dinner gathering with close friends, the recipes and time-saving tricks in this book will help you avoid stress, impress your guests, and enjoy your party.

chapter 1

strategies and tips for entertaining

A good party requires more than just good food. It's an exercise in making people happy, especially yourself. A stressed and frazzled host pretty much guarantees an unsuccessful party. So, think ahead: decide on the details for your party, and then figure out how to achieve your goals without losing your mind. If you have a slow cooker, take it out of hiding. If you don't have one, this is a great time to invest in one. This single appliance can help make your party a stress-free success!

The Big Picture

When thinking of how to please your guests, consider their senses: smell, taste, sound, sight, and touch. With some planning and thoughtfulness, you can choose the dishes you will cook, and the setting in which you'll present them, so your guests will find the combination a pleasant and comfortable experience. For example, they may not realize you chose the sound of soft Italian arias in the background to match the taste of Mrs. Bertolini's Tomato Sauce (page 112) and the scent of Mediterranean Coffee (page 255), but somehow that sauce will taste more authentically Italian and the coffee more aromatic. If you can satisfy as many as possible of your guests' five senses, then you will be on the right track. Since a slow cooker is so easy to use, you will find yourself with extra time to devote to the creation of a complete atmosphere.

the five senses

You might think taste is the most important sense when it comes to entertaining. But what is the first sensation you have when walking in the door to a party? Smell! Your guests' sense of smell will actually receive the first stimulation. Luckily, your slow cooker will be filling the house with warm aromas long before your guests even arrive. Still, be sure there is plenty of ventilation so it doesn't become too much of a good thing.

One key is to control what dishes are revealed, and when. Don't allow the desserts or dessert drinks to be uncovered until you're ready to serve them. This way, the aromas of dessert foods will not cloud those of the main course, and it will also help keep your guests in suspense.

Obviously, the next sense that comes into play when you're entertaining is taste. Finally, after arriving, making opening conversation, and sniffing the wonderful aromas wafting about, your guests will take their first tastes of each dish. Now the recipes and menu come under examination. Do the tastes of your dishes work well together? Perhaps more importantly, is there a variety? Some sweet, some salty, some savory, some tart? Variety and quality are your main concerns—not volume.

You don't have to do it all yourself, you know. Invite a few friends to help you cook. Let each choose her own contribution and have her bring her dish to the party. To give credit to the cooks, label each dish with the name of the person who prepared it and a fun fact about the item. This is also a great way for guests to get to know each other.

As for sound, music is a must—even if it is kept at a low volume. Choose something to match the food. If you're serving food from Latin America, you could play the vibrant flamenco nuevo styles of the Gipsy Kings. If the menu is simple and elegant, you might choose some classical music. Music gives your guests something to hear and enjoy as they indulge their other senses, and helps put them in the mood for whatever you're asking them to experience through taste. Your slow cookers will be silent, so they won't interfere.

The presentation of your dishes appeals to your guests' sense of sight. Color is a very important part of food presentation. A variety of colorful foods will intrigue your guests and add excitement to your atmosphere. If the foods you serve are generally all the same color, you can liven things up with garnishes or table decorations. Consider the colors of the foods you're preparing when you are planning the decorations for your serving areas.

Last, but not least, is the sense of touch. Though it may not seem so, touch is very important when preparing food. Your guests' hands will touch the dishware, glassware, cutlery, finger foods, and breads, and their mouths will be sensitive to the textures of the main dishes. Again, variety is a good idea. If you are serving a crunchy food, be sure to complement it with a soft, smooth dish.

Essential Equipment

The choices you make before you even start your party or event are very important. The slow-cooking equipment you have, for example, can make a huge difference in what you can provide for your guests, and how much work you will need to put in. You initially have to decide whether you will let the equipment already in your kitchen determine the menu, or if you will let the menu guide what additional equipment you will borrow or buy.

one slow cooker or six?

You might first decide on the menu, and then choose the number of slow cookers to match. If you have only two but you need five, you can buy the extras or borrow from friends. They will be more than willing to loan you their slow cookers when you point out that, as a thank you, you will return their appliances with a pint of leftover Brazilian Meat Stew (page 204) or Ginger Barbecue Beef (page 198).

QUESTION?

Is it okay to include a common ingredient in all the recipes for a party?
Yes—this can be a lot of fun! For example, try hosting a dinner party with a banana theme. You can prepare Banana Ribs (page 208), serve banana splits, and end the evening with a banana liqueur. Just be sure that none of your guests is allergic or opposed to your key ingredient.

Keep in mind that the slow cookers you use don't all have to be the same brand or size. Just be aware that different brands may work at different rates. It's always a good idea to test recipes in the designated slow cooker before the big day. Save the leftovers for yourself, or have them on hand as a backup in case your guests empty the pots on party day.

power thinking

When using slow cookers you should always consider electricity a piece of your equipment. Be sure you have enough of it! Do a brief trial run with all of the slow cookers you will be using, plugged in and running, while you also have on all of the lights, electronics, and air conditioning (or heaters) that you will be using during your party. Did you blow any fuses? You may need to be strategic about which outlets you use. The power demands in your kitchen may be near the limit already, but outlets in the living room may be on a separate fuse with capacity to spare. Just be sure to map out your electricity strategy long before your guests arrive.

Choosing a Good Party Menu

Your menu can shape your party, so you want to make sure it's a good one. Start by choosing what you want from your party. If you are making a Thanksgiving dinner, you likely want to provide comfort, tradition, and warmth. If you are throwing a birthday party for a unique friend, you might choose exotic spices, unusual dishes, and bright colors. Let your menu send a subtle message to your guests and help establish the mood.

main dishes

Your choice of one or two main dishes will set the tone for the entire menu. At most parties, you want people to mingle and circulate. To make sure people feel comfortable enough to move around, you can serve more main dishes and provide only small plates. That way, guests will be more likely to try the dishes in small portions, and they will get up from their seats more often.

Don't waste time trying to be good at everything. Choose one method of cooking, one kind of food, or one flavor you love and immerse yourself in it. If you like curry, for example, experiment with different curry recipes, learn the history of the cuisine, and host a curry party.

Though you may enjoy unusual foods, you should always include one or two classic dishes for the unadventurous. There will always be someone who would prefer a plain breast of chicken to a honey-smoked chicken wrap. If you're serving a rice dish, you might consider keeping a portion of plain rice aside for picky eaters. And if you're serving dishes with heavy sauces, you might want to keep the sauces on the side for optional use. If it isn't too much trouble, you'll be more likely to please everyone if you provide a few options for your timid guests.

salads and vegetables

Cold salads can add lovely color and texture to a meal, but some people also like vegetables cooked and savory. With slow cooking, the toughest vegetable material becomes soft and delicate. You can use your slow cooker to prepare vegetable dishes your guests might otherwise not experience. Mix vegetables with meats so each component picks up the flavor of the other. Or add vegetables to rice dishes to give them color and flavor.

One important thing to remember is that when you are serving fresh, cold salad, be sure to keep it a safe distance from your slow cookers. If the salad is too close to the hot appliance, you could accidentally steam your fresh greens! It's wise to keep fresh salads chilled until you are ready to serve them.

desserts and fruits

Though you might want to present your guests with elaborate homemade desserts, you will already be preparing a main course and might not have enough time. In this case, you can choose to serve a timeless classic: a variety of fruits. Your guests will never find these in the freezer case or at a fast-food restaurant; fruit makes a sweet, juicy treat. If you want to get creative, you can serve fruit with sauces or dips, and you can chill them or warm them slightly. If you want to make fruits one part of a larger dessert, you can have guests spoon them over ice cream or cake.

Be your own guest. Who is your party for, anyway? It's for you. Decide what you would like to eat, and then prepare it. Decide what you would like to experiment with, and then give it a try. Decide whose company you would enjoy, and then invite those people. Finally, relax and enjoy your evening.

If you do have more complex desserts planned, don't burden yourself with making too many. Choose one or two main desserts that you can complement with ice cream, fruit, or a warm beverage. Many guests will be too full from the main course to eat much dessert, so you need to make enough for only one to two servings per person. Some guests will want only a drink for dessert, such as coffee, tea, or hot cocoa, so you should have these choices on hand.

beverages

Many ideal party dishes can be made better with a nice, warm drink. Warm drinks keep guests soothed and comfortable, and they provide an aromatic excuse for conversation ("This smells marvelous! What is it?"). Warm beverages also offer a reason for slow sipping and pauses in conversation. A little bit of alcohol goes a long way when warmed, letting your guests enjoy the flavors without dulling their senses. Later in the evening, coffee-based drinks will pick people up and may even give your party a second wind.

Planning with the Slow Cooker

Once you have chosen your menu, you can start to take advantage of the benefits of slow cookers. You can plan your ingredient preparation, cooking schedules, and serving arrangements to work around your other party efforts. You can also adjust and adapt the recommended cooking times so you can coordinate the set of slow cooker recipes chosen for your menu. This will help your entertaining go more smoothly.

The beauty of slow cookers is their flexibility. No other form of cooking is so forgiving. For most dishes, a recommended setting of medium can be set lower for longer times or higher for shorter times. This means you can crank up the heat if you're running late, or turn it down, or even off, if there's a delay. Breads and puddings are the exception, since they require higher heat to ensure steaming and must be cooked at a high heat setting. Even with breads and puddings, though, a slow cooker on a low setting will keep things warm until the lid is removed for serving.

Dinner parties are great opportunities to use themes. For example, you could do a movie or TV show theme, or incorporate a detail about a favorite fictional character into the menu. This is an especially great idea for a child's celebration. In honor of Popeye, you could include spinach in every dish you prepare. As a reminder of Winnie the Pooh, you could use honey in all of your foods.

Another great strategy is to stagger the start and stop times for your recipes so appetizers and main dishes are ready earlier, desserts and drinks later. Automated timers can make this trick easier to perform. You can also manipulate the temperature settings to "force" multiple recipes to all fit your schedule. Do you have one recipe calling for eight hours on low, another for two hours on high, and another for four hours on low? Speed up the first by setting it on medium or high, slow down the second by getting a timer to delay the start time, and then they can all cook for four hours. To make them all fit an eight-hour time frame, use timers on the quicker recipes or, when compatible, simply turn them down and let them go longer. In most cases it won't hurt. Green vegetables and milk products may suffer with extended hours, so wait and add these more sensitive ingredients closer to serving time.

Serving from Slow Cookers

You should keep your slow cookers in mind as you are planning both your menu and your serving area. Can you make that dish in a slow cooker? Can you serve it from a slow cooker? Is there an electrical outlet near that serving table? Don't forget: you can use your slow cooker as a warming appliance, even for foods you purchased premade or prepared by other means. Once you've decided what to serve in your slow cookers, you can then think about where they should be placed. Also, consider whether they will need to be plugged in at that location or will require an extension cord.

the layout

The setup most conducive to slow-cooker foods is the buffet style. This way, the food can remain warm in the slow cookers and you will have plenty of room on your table for dishware, glassware, utensils, breads, spices, and condiments. You can choose either to set your table beforehand or to place a stack of dishes next to the slow cookers so guests can serve themselves.

FACT

It's nearly impossible to carry a drink, eat messy food, and mingle with people at the same time. Therefore, you need to make things easy for your guests. Be sure to provide them with plenty of seating, lots of napkins, and bite-size or neat foods. This way, everyone will feel more comfortable and there will be fewer spills in your home.

If you're using disposable dishware, you want to have a few waste receptacles placed discreetly around the eating area. If you do this, your guests will be able to throw out their used dishes and napkins and get new ones for other courses, and you will easily be able to remove clutter from the eating areas. If you are using china or other nondisposable dishware, either clear your guests' plates away as soon as they've finished, or show them where they can put things to make more space at the table.

Since you may have slow cookers for one or more of the courses, plan first where they will go, and then be sure chilled or frozen items (such as butter) stay a safe distance away from the heating appliances. It's also nice to have beverages and desserts on a separate table, so people can have more as they desire. Have a separate set of dishes, silverware, and napkins at each of these locations if you don't have a centralized area for dishes. Finally, make sure the tables are low enough so people can see what's in the slow cookers without leaning over them. You don't want your guests getting burned by the steam coming off your food.

the strategy

While most of your focus will fall on the food you're making and the atmosphere you're creating, you will need to implement some social strategy as well. Part of your goal is to keep your guests circulating and talking to one another throughout the party; thus, you don't want your serving area to be *too* efficient. Place the dessert far from the dinner dishes, and the beverages at still another end of the room. Have the plates and silverware at a separate location altogether.

QUESTION?

What are some creative activities to do at a dinner party?
Dinner parties are usually filled with a lot of talk. This can be fun, but if you want to give your party a little more excitement, you could try a variation. For example, you could have a trivia dinner party, in which people play trivia games while they eat. You could also try basic party games, like charades or Pictionary.

Also, remember that your guests are not actually starving, no matter what they say, and disregard the idea that you must provide them with food quickly. Your guests are there for entertainment, relaxation, and samples of all your delicious foods and beverages. The slower you "release" your dishes and allow the crowd to partake, the more suspense and topics of conversation you can provide.

Expand Your Horizons

There are a number of gadgets and knickknacks that can enhance the way you use your slow cooker. You may already have some of them lying around your house. The slow cooker has come a long way as far as design and innovation, but you can still adapt it further to fit your personal entertaining needs. Is there a drawer somewhere in your kitchen filled with odds and ends? If so, rummage through it—this might be the perfect opportunity to use some long-forgotten items.

timers

You probably have a timer somewhere in your kitchen or hardware drawer. If so, go find it! These simple devices can make your slow cooker even more user-friendly. Using a programmable timer to synchronize your slow cookers, or a cooking timer to alert yourself when the food is ready, will allow you to take a nap, read a book, or run an errand while you wait. If you don't already have one (or a few), go purchase some different kinds of inexpensive timers. If you choose cooking timers of different colors or those that make different sounds, you can use them to distinguish between your slow cookers. For example, set the blue timer for the Cinnamon Pear Cake (page 233) and the yellow timer for the Cream of Potato Soup (page 78), or set the ringing timer for the Royal Meatballs (page 22) and the buzzing timer for the Baked Apples (page 244). If you're willing to spend a little bit more money, you could purchase a programmable timer at a hardware store or one made specifically for use with a slow cooker. Some cookers have a computerized unit built-in that actually turns the slow cooker off when the time runs out. This way, you won't be interrupted during a well-deserved nap.

splitting up your slow cooker

Multichamber slow cookers offer the capability to have both an entree and an accompanying sauce at the same location. For example, if you're preparing a curry with a hot chutney, you can use a slow cooker with multiple chambers to separate the two. This will help you, as a host, keep track of the foods you've prepared, and it will also help your guests understand which foods go together. You can also use this tactic when making smaller volumes of several items, or to give your guests more options, as with toppings for ice cream or cakes.

One way to build your recipe collection is to borrow from friends. For a fun twist, put "BYOR" (Bring Your Own Recipe) on the invitation to your party and ask that each guest bring a note card with his favorite recipe written on it. Then you can put all the cards in a hat and have each guest choose one at random to try at home.

Another way to divide up your slow cooker is to use little glass or ceramic dishes within the appliance. By filling these dishes with batter or dough, you can prepare individual portions of steamed cakes and breads. Also, get some paper-lined foil sandwich sheets or keep a stack of double-thick foil sheets on hand to wrap sandwiches you'll steam. Gather a few trivets you can put in your slow cooker to stack those sandwiches or baking dishes. With these accessories on hand, your party planning and preparations will go much more smoothly.

Plan Ahead to Get Ahead

Since the slow cooker theme is efficiency, try to be efficient during every phase of your party planning. Think through your menu and ingredients to find ways to streamline your efforts. Be sure you have plenty of ingredients to avoid a last-minute trip to the store, prepare as much as possible ahead of time, and remember to make a little extra food for yourself. The time you spend planning will pay off along the way, leaving you a calmer and happier host on party day.

menu

Choose a menu with items you can prepare in advance. You may decide to simply prepare the ingredients for final assembly, or you may do the entire process, cooking and all, ahead of time. The hard part might be making space to freeze or refrigerate all of your foods until the day of the party. If this is the case, ask to store some food at a friend's or family member's house—just be sure this is someone you've invited to your party. If this option is not available, you may decide to change the menu based on what you can or can't get done the day before, or what will or won't fit in the refrigerator beforehand.

ingredients

Once you know the menu, you can make a consolidated shopping list. For example, you don't need 1 onion, ½ onion, and 2 onions—you need a bag of onions. Planning ahead like this can allow you to buy ingredients in bulk, which will save you money. Use consolidated thinking when you start preparing those ingredients, too. Instead of chopping onions at three separate times, chop them all at once and use as needed for your three recipes. You can do such steps a day or more in advance. Also, some raw ingredients, like chopped onions, can be frozen until needed.

ESSENTIAL

Planning ahead is one thing. Cooking ahead is even better. Plan your party menu so some of the dishes can be made days or even weeks ahead of time, then frozen or refrigerated. Sweet breads can be frozen for months and still taste freshly made; bread dough can be made ahead of time and frozen until the day before the party.

plan for you

Don't forget: This party is for you, too—not just for your guests. So, don't just make one batch of Got-to-Have-It Chocolate Sauce (page 47). As long as you've got the ingredients out, make a triple batch and plan on putting some in your own refrigerator or freezer before the guests arrive. You might not have time to enjoy it during your party, or your guests might gobble it up before you get a taste. But this way, you can rest easy, knowing you've got a batch set aside you can enjoy, perhaps while you're cleaning up the next day.

Start the Party Early

Is "work" the first word that comes to mind when you decide to have a party? If so, clear your mind of the thought. You don't have to do it alone. Instead, get some friends to help you throw your party. Let them choose their own roles and help before, during, and after the party, and you can all walk away having done less work and enjoyed yourselves more. This is an especially great strategy if you're entertaining with slow cookers—you can pool your equipment resources together to increase your party possibilities.

One way to spoil a recipe is to get halfway through and realize you're missing a key ingredient. To avoid this, gather and prepare your ingredients before starting so that no surprises pop up while you're cooking. If you should realize you've forgotten something, it's helpful to have a friend nearby who doesn't mind running errands for you.

the party before the party

Why not make the party preparation an event within itself? Choose a date before the big event and invite several friends over to help prepare. What's their motivation to help you out? It's a chance to get out of their homes, spend time with good friends, and contribute to a fantastic event. You could even throw in an extra incentive for your helpers, such as a small gift or leftover food from the party. Having friends help with preparations will also give you a chance to store premade foods in their refrigerators until the day of the event.

keep it relaxed

Your friends will not feel comfortable helping with your party if you are bossy and domineering. Although you will feel some pressure as the host of your event, try to remain calm and let your friends help you in any way they'd like. You may find you have a friend willing to run quick errands, another friend with excellent chopping skills, and still another who is good at decorating. Perhaps you have a photographer friend who doesn't like to cook but can snap candid photos during the big event. If you're really lucky, you'll find you have a friend who prefers cleaning to cooking. Here are some other tasks you can divvy up with friends:

- Providing more equipment
- Organizing the guest list and invitations
- Preparing music or other entertainment
- Greeting guests and taking coats
- Serving or bartending

With friends involved, you can share the work of the party as well as the rewards. In addition to the fun of bringing people together, you can plan your menu so there are plenty of leftovers to share. Yes, there is a lot involved in making a party run well. But the more help you have, the more fun you will all have together. And slow cookers will make the job easier on everyone.

chapter 2
finger foods and snacks

Hot Western BBQ Ribs

*Be sure to provide plenty of napkins for your guests,
and don't serve this in a room with white carpet!*

Serves 6

Cooking time: 4–6 hours
Preparation time: 15 minutes
Attention: Minimal
Pot size: 3–5 quarts

3 pounds beef short ribs
1 onion
1 clove garlic
1 cup catsup
½ cup water
¼ cup brown sugar
*3 tablespoons Worcestershire
    sauce*
1 teaspoon salt
2 teaspoons mustard

1. Cut the ribs into serving-size portions.

2. Arrange the ribs in the slow cooker.

3. Mince the onion and garlic. Combine with the other ingredients and pour the mixture over the ribs.

4. Cover and heat on a low setting for 4 to 6 hours.

Pizza Party

Homemade pizza, anyone? At some Italian bakeries you can buy ready-to-use servings of frozen pizza dough. Thaw it, let it rise, spin it in the air, bring out the pizza sauce, and let your guests do the work. Just be sure you have cheese and toppings ready.

Toasty Spiced Almonds

See if you can find different brands of curry spice in international markets near you. You can also substitute roasted soy nuts for almonds.

Yields about 3 cups

Cooking time: 3–4 hours
Preparation time: 15 minutes
Attention: Minimal
Pot size: 3–5 quarts

2 tablespoons butter
1 tablespoon curry powder
½ teaspoon seasoned salt
1 pound blanched almonds

1. Melt the butter in a saucepan over low heat. Add the curry powder and seasoned salt and mix well.

2. Put the almonds in the slow cooker and add the butter mixture, stirring to coat all of the nuts.

3. Cover and heat on a low setting for 2 to 3 hours.

4. An hour before serving, uncover and heat on a high setting. Set on low heat for serving.

Meatballs with Mushrooms

Cooking time: 3–4 hours
Preparation time: 60 minutes
Attention: Minimal
Pot size: 3–5 quarts

1 clove garlic
1 pound ground beef
¼ cup chopped celery
½ cup uncooked rice
½ cup bread crumbs
½ teaspoon sage
½ teaspoon white pepper
½ teaspoon salt
2 tablespoons vegetable oil
½ pound mushrooms
1 onion
2 tablespoons vegetable oil
1 tablespoon flour
1 cup water
1 cup tomato sauce

Serve these meatballs with skewers or, for a more substantial dish, provide rolls and let your guests make little meatball sandwiches.

1. Crush and mince the garlic. Combine the meat, garlic, and celery with the rice, crumbs, spices, and salt.

2. Form into ¾-inch balls. Brown in 2 tablespoons vegetable oil in a pan over medium heat and drain. Arrange in the slow cooker.

3. Mince the mushrooms and onion. Sauté the mushrooms and onion in 2 tablespoons vegetable oil. Add the flour to the mushroom mixture and stir to thicken. Add the water and tomato sauce to this slowly and mix until smooth.

4. Pour the tomato and mushroom mixture over balls.

5. Cover and heat on a low setting for 3 to 4 hours.

Rice and Slow Cooking
Rice is nice, especially when it's made in a slow cooker. Use converted rice (not instant) and it will come out light and fluffy. You can also add vegetables and spices to the rice for an easy meal.

Grandpa Riley's Tamales

*If you aren't able to get small heads of baby cabbage
for the tamale wrappers, use large leaves cut in half.
You can also try this with red cabbage, or a mixture of both.*

1. Coarsely grind pork. Mix with rice, salt, and pepper.

2. Place 2 tablespoons of the meat mixture in each cabbage leaf and roll, tucking under the ends.

3. Arrange the rolls tightly in the slow cooker.

4. Mince the garlic. Mix chili powder, tomatoes, garlic, and water; pour over cabbage rolls. Place an inverted glass plate or baking dish on top of the rolls to hold them in place.

5. Cover and cook on medium setting for 4 to 5 hours.

Cabbage Roll Trick
When making cabbage rolls in a slow cooker, put them on a bed of cabbage scraps to keep them off the base of the crockery dish. You can always freeze the cabbage base and use it later in a soup or stew.

Yields 48

Cooking time: 4–5 hours
Preparation time: 90 minutes
Attention: Minimal
Pot size: 3–5 quarts

1½ pounds pork
1½ cups cooked rice
1 tablespoon salt
1 tablespoon pepper
48 small cabbage leaves
2 cloves garlic
3 tablespoons chili powder
2½ cups cubed tomatoes
1 cup water

Royal Meatballs

Cooking time: 3–4 hours
Preparation time: 60 minutes
Attention: Minimal
Pot size: 3–5 quarts

1 onion
6 shallots
3 tablespoons butter
½ pound lamb
½ pound veal
½ pound bacon
1 small bunch parsley
12 anchovies
¼ cup chives
1 clove garlic
½ teaspoon salt
¼ teaspoon pepper
¼ teaspoon nutmeg
⅛ teaspoon cayenne pepper
½ cup water
2 eggs
3 cups Regal Caper Sauce
    (page 50)

These flavorful meatballs are prepared with Regal Caper Sauce (page 50).
Serve them either skewered, as an appetizer, or with slices of minipumpernickel.

1. Mince the onion and shallots, then sauté in the butter in a pan over medium heat until soft. Transfer the onion and shallots to a mixing bowl and set aside the pan with remaining butter.

2. Coarsely grind or mince the meat. Finely chop the parsley, anchovies, and chives. Crush the garlic and then mince it.

3. Combine all ingredients except Regal Caper Sauce with the onion mixture in the mixing bowl and mix well. Form into ¾-inch balls; heat the meatballs in the pan over medium heat until browned, then drain.

4. Arrange the meatballs in the slow cooker and cover with Regal Caper Sauce.

5. Cover and heat on a low setting for 3 to 4 hours.

Watch Your Wiring
Before or after cooking, don't put your slow cooker in the refrigerator unless the crockery is removable and can go in alone. Otherwise the electrical components may rust and leave you needing a whole new appliance.

Paprika Meatballs

*These can be served with skewers as a finger food
or over pasta as a main dish. They are excellent with fresh angel hair pasta.*

1. Coarsely grind the meat. Crush and mince the garlic; grate or finely dice the cheese.

2. Combine the meat, garlic, and cheese in a mixing bowl with the eggs, paprika, salt, crumbs, and milk; mix well.

3. Form into ¾-inch balls and sauté in oil in a pan over medium heat until browned. Drain and arrange the meatballs in the slow cooker.

4. Dice the tomatoes. Pour the tomatoes and tomato sauce over the meatballs.

5. Cover and heat on a low setting for 3 to 4 hours.

Pasta and Slow Cooking

Pasta is a great addition to slow-cooked meals, but it should not be made in your slow cooker. To serve pasta with a dish, cook the pasta separately, then serve on the side, or add it to the slow cooker just before serving. If the pasta is coated with a little butter or oil, it can be kept warm by itself in a slow cooker.

Serves 8

Cooking time: 3–4 hours
Preparation time: 60 minutes
Attention: Minimal
Pot size: 3–5 quarts

1 pound veal
1 pound pork
1 clove garlic
¼ pound Mozzarella cheese
3 eggs
1 tablespoon paprika
1 teaspoon salt
1 cup bread crumbs
½ cup milk
2 tablespoons vegetable oil
2 tomatoes
1 cup tomato sauce

Sweet Ham Balls

You don't need to add salt in this recipe; the ham should provide just enough.
As a variation, try substituting ¼ cup molasses for the brown sugar.

Serves 12

Cooking time: 3–4 hours
Preparation time: 45 minutes
Attention: Minimal
Pot size: 3–5 quarts

1 pound ground beef
1 pound ground ham
2 eggs
1 cup graham cracker crumbs
1 cup milk
¼ cup canola or corn oil
½ teaspoon pepper
2 cups tomato sauce
½ cup brown sugar
1 cup vinegar
2 teaspoons dry mustard

1. Mix the beef, ham, eggs, crumbs, milk, and pepper. Form into ¾-inch balls and sauté in oil in a pan over medium heat until browned.

2. Drain the meatballs and arrange in the slow cooker.

3. Mix the tomato sauce, brown sugar, vinegar, and mustard; pour over the balls.

4. Cover and heat on a low setting for 3 to 4 hours.

Bob's Beer Sausages

Sometimes the simple things in life are the best! Keep some browned, cut sausages in the freezer, ready to slow cook for a quick halftime treat.

1. Heat the sausages in a pan over medium heat until browned. Drain and cut them into bite-size pieces.

2. Combine the browned sausage with the beer in the slow cooker.

3. Cover and heat on a low setting for 2 to 3 hours.

Serves 12

Cooking time: 2–3 hours
Preparation time: 15 minutes
Attention: Minimal
Pot size: 3–5 quarts

3 pounds spicy Italian pork sausages
2 bottles beer

Sweet Nuts

Try substituting your favorite nuts in this recipe. Use them in combinations, unless using peanuts, which have an overpowering flavor.

1. Remove any scraps of shell from the nuts and transfer them to the slow cooker.

2. Mix the sugar, salt, and spices in a mixing bowl.

3. Beat the egg white until stiff, and then add the water to the egg white.

4. Sprinkle the egg mixture over the nuts. While the nuts are still moist, sprinkle the sugar mixture over the nuts, stirring well.

5. Cover and heat on a low setting for 3 to 4 hours. Stir the mixture 2 or 3 times.

Yields about 2 cups

Cooking time: 3–4 hours
Preparation time: 15 minutes
Attention: Minimal
Pot size: 3–5 quarts

1 cup walnuts
1 cup almonds
½ cup sugar
½ teaspoon salt
¼ teaspoon cinnamon
¼ teaspoon cloves
¼ teaspoon allspice
1 egg white
2 tablespoons water

Sweet Buttermilk Meatballs

Serves 8

Cooking time: 2–3 hours
Preparation time: 60 minutes
Attention: Minimal
Pot size: 3–5 quarts

1 onion
2 pounds ground beef
1 cup bread crumbs
½ cup milk
1 teaspoon salt
¼ teaspoon pepper
3 tablespoons butter
¼ cup butter
¼ cup flour
2¼ cups buttermilk
2 tablespoons sugar
¼ teaspoon salt
⅛ teaspoon pepper
1½ teaspoons dry mustard
1 egg

*Serve this with a sprinkle of diced sweet red pepper for a garnish.
It will add color, as well as a nice dash of flavor!*

1. Mince the onion. Mix the onion, ground beef, bread crumbs, milk, salt, and pepper. Form into ¾-inch balls.

2. Sauté the balls in 3 tablespoons butter in a pan over medium heat until browned; drain, discarding the grease. Transfer the meatballs to the slow cooker.

3. Add the remaining butter to the pan and melt it over low heat. Stir in the flour until well blended.

4. Slowly add the buttermilk to the flour mixture; blend well. Add the sugar, salt, spices, and egg; stir over low heat to thicken. Pour the sauce over the meatballs in the slow cooker.

5. Cover and heat on a low setting for 2 to 3 hours.

Thermostat Alert

Plan for steam. Once all of those slow cookers are opened up, the steamy aromas may warm up your party rooms. Be sure you have enough ventilation or air conditioning to keep the temperature and humidity comfortable for your guests.

Sherry Meatballs

When serving these as finger foods,
be sure to include small slices of French bread to soak up the rich sauce.

1. Heat the bacon in a pan over medium heat until browned. Remove the browned slices from the pan to drain; set aside most of the bacon fat to use later.

2. Dice the onion and garlic. Sauté the onion and garlic in the remaining bacon fat, then remove the onion mixture from the pan and add it to the bread crumbs, beef, eggs, salt, and spices in a mixing bowl. Form the meat mixture into ¾-inch balls. Sauté the balls in the bacon fat you set aside over medium heat; drain. Crumble the bacon; arrange the meatballs in the slow cooker with the crumbled bacon.

3. Slice the mushrooms. Sauté in butter in a pan over medium heat until browned; stir in the flour and allow the juices to thicken. Slowly stir in the milk and water. Pour the thickened mushroom sauce over the meatballs in the slow cooker.

4. Cover and heat on a low setting for 2 to 3 hours.

5. Half an hour before serving, add the sherry.

Meatball Mayhem

No one wants to spend hours forming meatballs. Instead, use an ice cream scoop. You can even get scoops in different sizes, so you can churn out petite or jumbo meatballs in no time.

Serves 8

Cooking time: 3–4 hours
Preparation time: 60 minutes
Attention: Minimal
Pot size: 3–5 quarts

6 slices bacon
2 onions
2 cloves garlic
1 cup dry bread crumbs
2 pounds ground beef
2 eggs
1 teaspoon salt
½ teaspoon pepper
½ teaspoon oregano
1 pound mushrooms
3 tablespoons butter
2 tablespoons flour
½ cup milk
½ cup water
½ cup sherry

Spicy Walnuts

*For a more exotic treat, substitute hazelnuts or pecans for the walnuts
in this recipe, or use a combination of nuts other than peanuts. Serve hot.*

Yields about 4 cups

Cooking time: 3–4 hours
Preparation time: 30 minutes
Attention: Minimal
Pot size: 3–5 quarts

1 pound walnut meats
½ teaspoon onion powder
1 teaspoon salt
¼ teaspoon garlic powder
¼ cup vegetable oil

1. Combine the ingredients in the slow cooker.

2. Cover and heat on a low setting for 3 to 4 hours. Stir occasionally.

Chili Nuts

*This quickie recipe uses a seasoning mix shortcut, but you can replace it with
your own favorite chili seasoning combination if you wish.*

Yields about 5 cups

Cooking time: 3–4 hours
Preparation time: 15 minutes
Attention: Minimal
Pot size: 3–5 quarts

¼ cup butter
1 package chili seasoning mix
1½ pounds shelled peanuts

1. Melt the butter in a saucepan over low heat. Add the chili seasoning and mix well.

2. Put the peanuts in the slow cooker and add the butter mixture, stirring to coat all of the nuts.

3. Cover and heat on a low setting for 2 to 3 hours.

4. Half an hour before serving, uncover and heat on a high setting. Set on low heat for serving.

Tangy Burgundy Ribs

You can serve this as a finger food, or with rice as a more substantial dish. Don't forget to include plenty of napkins!

Serves 8

Cooking time: 5–6 hours
Preparation time: 30 minutes
Attention: Minimal
Pot size: 3–5 quarts

4 pounds lean short ribs
½ cup flour
*¼ teaspoon coarsely ground
   black pepper*
2 tablespoons oil
4 stalks celery
2 onions
*3 teaspoons prepared
   mustard*
*2 tablespoons Worcestershire
   sauce*
1 teaspoon salt
1 cup catsup
½ cup wine vinegar
1 cup Burgundy wine

1. Cut the ribs into serving-size pieces. Mix the flour and pepper and use to lightly coat the ribs.

2. Heat the ribs in oil in a pan over medium heat until browned, and then drain.

3. Slice the celery and onions. Combine with the meat, mustard, Worcestershire sauce, salt, catsup, and vinegar in the slow cooker.

4. Cover and heat on a medium setting for 4 to 5 hours. Half an hour before serving, add the wine to the slow cooker.

Protect Your Slow Cooker
When the party's over, don't forget to let your slow cookers cool before you fill them with dishwater. If they're still hot when you add the water, they could crack. Once they've cooled and you've added water, you might want to let them soak overnight to loosen any hardened foods.

Burgundy Pepper Beef

*You can serve this with small forks, or provide your guests
with small bowls of warm egg noodles to enjoy with the sauce.*

Serves 8

Cooking time: 4–5 hours
Preparation time: 45 minutes
Attention: Moderate
Pot size: 3–5 quarts

*2 pounds stew beef, such
    as blade roast or chuck
    steak*
½ cup flour
½ teaspoon black pepper
2 tablespoons oil
2 onions
½ pound mushrooms
*1 tablespoon Worcestershire
    sauce*
½ teaspoon salt
1 tablespoon sugar
1 cup water
½ cup vinegar
2 tablespoons flour
1 cup Burgundy wine

1. Cube the beef. Mix the flour and pepper. Use the flour mixture to coat the beef cubes. Heat the meat in oil in a pan over medium heat until browned. Transfer the beef to the slow cooker, but keep the oil in the pan.

2. Quarter the onions and halve the mushrooms. Sauté the onions and mushrooms over medium heat in the pan in the oil used for the beef, until the onion mixture is soft.

3. Put the beef, onions, mushrooms, Worcestershire sauce, salt, sugar, water, and vinegar in the slow cooker.

4. Cover and heat on a low setting for 3 to 4 hours.

5. An hour before serving, take 2 tablespoons of sauce from the slow cooker and let it cool briefly before mixing it well with the remaining flour. Stir this into the sauce in the slow cooker, mixing well. Add the Burgundy.

Be Cool, But Not Too Cool

Don't add icy cold ingredients to a preheated slow cooker. Sudden temperature changes can crack the crockery pot. That's a surprise you definitely don't want on the day of your party.

Imperial Meatballs

Serve with chopsticks. To be kind, provide pointed ones so your guests can use them to skewer their food, in case they're not chopstick users.

1. Finely chop the onion. Peel and cut the chestnuts into fine strips. Combine with the ground beef, eggs, crumbs, and pepper and form into ¾-inch balls.

2. Sauté the balls in oil in a pan over high heat until browned, then drain and arrange them in the slow cooker.

3. Crush and slice the garlic and distribute over the meatballs. Combine the soy sauce, ginger, and sugar in a mixing bowl, and then pour over the meatballs and garlic in the slow cooker.

4. Cover and heat on a low setting for 3 to 4 hours.

Serves 8

Cooking time: 3–4 hours
Preparation time: 45 minutes
Attention: Minimal
Pot size: 3–5 quarts

1 onion
¼ cup water chestnuts
2 pounds ground beef
4 eggs
1 cup bread crumbs
1 teaspoon pepper
2 tablespoons sesame oil
4 cloves garlic
2 cups soy sauce
4 teaspoons ground ginger
½ cup sugar

Hawaiian Hillbillies

Serves 12

Cooking time: 3–4 hours
Preparation time: 30 minutes
Attention: Minimal
Pot size: 3–5 quarts

3 pounds link sausages
2 pounds fresh pineapple,
    peeled, cored, and cubed
¼ cup brown sugar
¼ cup cornstarch
1 cup water
½ cup brown sugar
1 tablespoon prepared
    mustard
1 tablespoon soy sauce

This sweet and savory dish works well using smoked sausages.
If using canned pineapple, delete the ¼ cup of brown sugar.

1. Sauté the sausage in a pan over medium heat until browned. Drain and cut into bite-size pieces; if using cocktail-size link sausages, leave whole.

2. Arrange the pineapple in the slow cooker with the sausages. Sprinkle with ¼ cup brown sugar while arranging in the slow cooker.

3. Blend the cornstarch with water.

4. Add ½ cup brown sugar, mustard, and soy sauce to the cornstarch mixture and blend well. Pour the brown sugar mixture over the sausage and pineapple in the slow cooker.

5. Cover and heat on a low setting for 3 to 4 hours.

Making Croutons

Don't throw away that stale bread. Make croutons! Any type of bread will work. Brush it with oil or melted butter, cut it into cubes, sprinkle on some herbs and cheese, broil until browned, and pop in the freezer. A quick toasting later gives you an instant garnish.

Homemade Tamales

For a more authentic feel, you can use shredded beef or pork
to substitute for the ground beef in this recipe.

1. If using dried husks, soak them in warm water for 2 hours to soften before using. Alternatively, fresh husks should be laid out on trays and lightly dried overnight, uncovered, or heated for several hours in a 150°F oven.

2. Simmer the meat with the cumin in 2½ cups water until cooked. Drain and set aside meat; save 1½ cups of the liquid. After the liquid cools, use a large spoon to skim off any solidified fat; discard the fat.

3. Cut the lard into the cornmeal, baking powder, and salt. Slowly add the set-aside meat broth and mix well into the cornmeal mixture.

4. Lay out the husks on a flat surface. On the smooth side of each husk, spread about 1½ tablespoons of the cornmeal dough. Top with about ¾ tablespoon of meat. Fold the dough around the meat. Roll the husk around the dough and tie it with a string around the middle of the bundle. Arrange the bundles on a trivet or rack in the slow cooker, and pour water around the base.

5. Cover and heat on a high setting for 3 to 4 hours.

Yields about 20

Cooking time: 3–4 hours
Preparation time: 2 hours
Attention: Minimal
Pot size: 3–5 quarts

½ pound corn husks
½ pound spicy pork sausage
½ pound ground beef
1 teaspoon cumin
2½ cups water
½ cup lard (or shortening)
2 cups cornmeal
2 teaspoons baking powder
½ teaspoon salt
String
1 cup water

Spicy Plum Chicken

Serves 6

Cooking time: 3–4 hours
Preparation time: 30 minutes
Attention: Minimal
Pot size: 3–5 quarts

2 pounds boneless chicken
½ teaspoon white pepper
½ teaspoon ground ginger
½ teaspoon cinnamon
¼ teaspoon ground cloves
1 tablespoon soy sauce
3 tablespoons soy sauce
2 tablespoons honey
½ cup plum jelly
2 teaspoons sugar
2 teaspoons vinegar
¼ cup chutney

Fresh plums can add a nice twist to this recipe. Throw in six (without the pits), with ¼ cup sugar. Leave off the lid for the last half hour to condense the sauce.

1. Cut the chicken into serving-size pieces. Mix the spices and divide the spice mixture in half. Sprinkle the chicken with half of this mixture.

2. To the other half of the spice mixture, add 1 tablespoon soy sauce. Sprinkle this over the chicken, as well. Refrigerate the chicken for 4 hours or overnight.

3. Arrange the chicken pieces in the slow cooker.

4. Mix the remaining 3 tablespoons of soy sauce with the honey, jelly, sugar, vinegar, and chutney. Dribble this mixture over the chicken pieces in the slow cooker.

5. Cover and heat on a low setting for 3 to 4 hours.

Clean Cutting

Is your bread too soft to cut cleanly? Chill or lightly freeze bread before cutting. This especially helps when cutting with cookie cutters. Another tip is to make sure the bread is at least 24 hours old, and the knife is serrated.

chapter 3
dips, fondues, and sauces

Buttery Butterscotch Sauce

A good sauce will dress up even the simplest ice cream.
Spoon this over classic vanilla ice cream for a delectable treat.

Yields about 3 cups

Cooking time: 2–3 hours
Preparation time: 30 minutes
Attention: Minimal
Pot size: 3–5 quarts

2 cups brown sugar
¼ cup flour
¼ teaspoon cinnamon
½ teaspoon salt
2 cups water
¼ cup butter
1 teaspoon vanilla

1. Combine the brown sugar, flour, cinnamon, and salt in a mixing bowl. Boil the water in a saucepan over high heat.

2. Add the brown sugar mixture to the boiling water and mix for 5 minutes while stirring over a low heat.

3. Transfer the brown sugar mixture to the slow cooker and heat 1 to 2 hours on a low setting.

4. An hour before serving, add the butter and vanilla.

The Party Cure

Do you hate to cook? Have a party! Fill those slow cookers to the brim, and then freeze the leftovers. This way, you won't have to cook for quite a while, but you'll still be a generous host in the eyes of your guests.

Creamed Cheese Beef Dip

*Use real Parmesan cheese, chipped from a block, for this dish.
It's the little things that make the difference your guests will sense!*

1. Chop the onion and finely mince the garlic.

2. Sauté the beef with onion and garlic in a pan over medium heat until the meat is browned.

3. Add the tomato sauce and catsup to the meat mixture. Simmer 5 minutes, then collect surface fat with a spoon and discard.

4. Combine the meat mixture with oregano, sugar, and cheeses in the slow cooker.

5. Cover and heat on a low setting for 2 to 3 hours.

Serves 8

Cooking time: 2–3 hours
Preparation time: 45 minutes
Attention: Minimal
Pot size: 3–5 quarts

1 onion
1 clove garlic
1 pound ground beef
1 cup tomato sauce
¼ cup catsup
1 teaspoon oregano
1 teaspoon sugar
½ pound cream cheese
¼ pound Parmesan cheese

Tangy Crab Dip

Cooking time: 2–3 hours
Preparation time: 30 minutes
Attention: Minimal
Pot size: 3–5 quarts

6 ounces crabmeat
8 ounces cream cheese
1 tablespoon milk
½ teaspoon horseradish
¼ teaspoon salt
¼ teaspoon pepper
¼ cup toasted almonds

*For a little extra kick, add more horseradish than this recipe calls for.
If you're really adventurous, try doubling the horseradish measurement.*

1. Shred the crabmeat. Cut the cream cheese into cubes. Combine all ingredients except almonds in the slow cooker.

2. Cover and heat on a low setting for 2 to 3 hours.

3. Before serving, sprinkle the dip with the almonds as a garnish.

Leftovers to Go

Spread the wealth. Set out "to go" containers for your guests and they'll help take care of those pesky leftovers. And take notice of which foods they bring home—these are the dishes they really enjoyed.

Spicy Mexican Beef Dip

*Serve with tortilla chips as a dip or with rolls to make sandwiches,
with some romaine lettuce and chips on the side.*

1. Chop the onion. Sauté the meat with the onion and chili powder in a pan over medium heat until the meat is browned. Drain the fat and transfer the meat mixture to the slow cooker.

2. Slice the olives and pit if necessary. Crush the kidney beans. Add the olives, beans, catsup, and salt to the slow cooker.

3. Cover and heat on a low setting for 2 to 3 hours.

4. Before serving, shred the cheese and provide as garnish.

Serves 6

Cooking time: 2–3 hours
Preparation time: 45 minutes
Attention: Minimal
Pot size: 3–5 quarts

1 onion
1 pound ground beef
1½ teaspoons chili powder
½ cup black olives
2 cups cooked kidney beans
½ cup catsup
½ teaspoon salt
½ pound Monterey Jack cheese

Peppy Cheddar Dip

*Try this with other cheeses or different dried meats such as prosciutto.
Provide halved or whole red cherry tomatoes as a garnish.*

1. Dice or shred the cheese, and finely mince the chilies.

2. Slice the pepperoni, then cut it into strips. Pit and dice the olives.

3. Combine all the ingredients in the slow cooker.

4. Cover and heat on a low setting for 2 to 3 hours, or until all the cheese is melted and the mixture is bubbling.

Serves 16

Cooking time: 2–3 hours
Preparation time: 30 minutes
Attention: Minimal
Pot size: 3–5 quarts

1 pound mozzarella cheese
1 pound Cheddar cheese
¼ cup green chilies
½ pound pepperoni
½ cup black olives
2 cups mayonnaise

Chili con Queso

Here's a simple recipe for a tasty party dip.
This dip freezes well, and it's also great on potatoes!

Serves 16

Cooking time: 2–3 hours
Preparation time: 45 minutes
Attention: Minimal
Pot size: 3–5 quarts

2 pounds ground beef
2 pounds Monterey Jack
*   cheese*
2 onions
4 ounces chili peppers
1 pound tomatoes
½ teaspoon cumin
2 tablespoons chopped fresh
*   cilantro*

1. Sauté the meat in a pan over medium heat until brown, then drain and transfer meat to the slow cooker.

2. Slice or cube the cheese, dice the onions and chilies, and coarsely chop the tomatoes.

3. Add the cut ingredients and cumin to the slow cooker and heat on low setting for 2 to 3 hours. Stir to mix as the cheese melts.

4. Before serving, add the cilantro to the mixture as a garnish. Do not heat covered longer than four hours or cheese may separate.

Using Shredded Meats
Any time a recipe calls for ground beef, you might want to substitute some shredded beef instead. Use leftover roasts or steak and shred the meat yourself. This will give your dishes a great new texture.

Creamy Parmesan Fondue

Use this either as a sauce or a fondue.
You can spoon it over pasta, vegetables, or meats, or use it for dipping.

Yields about 5 cups

Cooking time: 3–4 hours
Preparation time: 30 minutes
Attention: Minimal
Pot size: 3–5 quarts

1 pound cream cheese
2 cups milk
2 cloves garlic
¼ onion
½ pound Parmesan cheese
½ teaspoon salt
½ teaspoon pepper

1. Cut the cream cheese into cubes and place in the slow cooker.

2. Cover and heat on a low setting for 1 hour or until the cream cheese is melted. Stir in the milk until blended.

3. Mince the garlic. Finely slice the onion. Grate the Parmesan cheese. Add the garlic, onion, Parmesan, salt, and pepper to slow cooker.

4. Cover and heat on a low setting for 2 to 3 hours.

Old-Timer Cocoa Sauce

Provide bowls of shaved or chipped chocolate for any guests who are extreme chocolate lovers. Try this sauce over cake or ice cream.

Yields about 4 cups

Cooking time: 2–4 hours
Preparation time: 15 minutes
Attention: Minimal
Pot size: 3–5 quarts

2 cups chocolate chips
½ cup butter
½ cup cocoa
1½ cups sugar
¼ teaspoon salt
1½ cups light cream
1 teaspoon vanilla

1. Put the chocolate chips and butter in the slow cooker.

2. Cover and heat on low setting for 1 to 2 hours.

3. When the chocolate and butter are melted, add the remaining ingredients to the slow cooker.

4. Cover and heat on a low setting for 1 to 2 hours.

Better Chocolate

If chocolate chips are too mundane for you, try using your favorite chocolate candies or baking chocolates in your recipes. These will deliver a much richer flavor for more decadent desserts.

Banana Sauce Flambé

*It can't get much better than sweet, buttery food that is also dramatic!
Just be sure to use caution when flaming the sauce.*

1. Diagonally slice the bananas into 1-inch-thick slices. Sauté in butter and brown sugar in a pan over low heat until bananas are translucent.

2. Arrange the bananas in the slow cooker. Sprinkle the bananas with the orange zest, cinnamon, and lime juice.

3. Cover and heat on a low setting for 2 to 3 hours.

4. Before serving, heat the rum in a saucepan over low heat until it begins to steam. Pour it over the surface of the banana mixture and light.

Serves 6

Cooking time: 2–3 hours
Preparation time: 45 minutes
Attention: Moderate
Pot size: 3–5 quarts

6 ripe bananas
¼ cup butter
3 tablespoons brown sugar
Zest of ½ orange
¼ teaspoon cinnamon
2 tablespoons lime juice
½ cup rum

Brandied Chocolate Fondue

*You don't need a double boiler to melt chocolate if you have a slow cooker.
That alone is an excuse for a chocolate party.*

1. Combine all ingredients (except cream and cake) in the slow cooker.

2. Cover and cook on high for 15 to 20 minutes, or until chocolate melts.

3. Add the cream and stir. Heat on a low setting for 1 to 2 hours.

4. Before serving, cut the cake into sizes suitable for dipping.

Serves 10

Cooking time: 2–3 hours
Preparation time: 30 minutes
Attention: Minimal
Pot size: 3–5 quarts

12 squares unsweetened
chocolate
2 cups sugar
1 cup butter
½ teaspoon salt
¼ cup brandy
1 cup heavy cream
1 pound dense cake

Sweet Curried Fruit

This is great hot or cold with desserts, or even with meats!
Try some mixed into chicken salad or spooned over a slice of ham.

Serves 20

Cooking time: 3–4 hours
Preparation time: 45 minutes
Attention: Minimal
Pot size: 3–5 quarts

⅓ *cup butter*
¾ *cup brown sugar*
4 teaspoons curry powder
1 pound pears
1 pound peaches
1 pound apricots
2 pounds pineapple

1. Melt the butter in a saucepan over low heat. Add the brown sugar and curry powder, mixing well until blended.

2. Cut the fruit, fresh or canned, into bite-size pieces and place in the slow cooker.

3. Spoon the curry mixture over the top of the fruit.

4. Cover and heat on a low setting for 3 to 4 hours.

Brandy Sauce

You can refrigerate this sauce for up to a week. This allows you to prepare it
well in advance, which is especially helpful when planning a party.

Yields about 5 cups

Cooking time: 3–4 hours
Preparation time: 30 minutes
Attention: Minimal
Pot size: 3–5 quarts

2 cups dried apricots
2 cups water
1 cup sugar
1 cup brandy

1. Dice the apricots. (Fresh apricots may be substituted for dried; use twice the volume of fruit, remove pits, and add only ½ cup water.)

2. Combine with other ingredients in the slow cooker.

3. Cover and heat on a low setting for 3 to 4 hours.

Vanilla Butter Sauce

If you have access to vanilla beans,
drop one in while this is cooking for a richer flavor.

1. Combine all ingredients in the slow cooker.

2. Cover and cook on a low setting for 1 hour, then stir to mix.

3. Continue to heat on a low setting for another 1 to 2 hours.

Yields about 1½ cups

Cooking time: 2–3 hours
Preparation time: 30 minutes
Attention: Minimal
Pot size: 3–5 quarts

½ cup cream
½ cup butter
1 cup sugar
1½ teaspoons vanilla

Creamy Pecan Beef Dip

Try this with thin slices of French baguettes to make tiny sandwiches.
Provide plenty of bread—these will go quickly!

1. Finely shred the smoked beef.

2. Combine all ingredients in the slow cooker.

3. Cover and heat on a low setting for 2 to 3 hours or until dip bubbles at edges. Do not overheat.

Serves 6

Cooking time: 2–3 hours
Preparation time: 30 minutes
Attention: Minimal
Pot size: 3–5 quarts

3 ounces sliced smoked beef
2 tablespoons finely chopped
  onion
½ cup finely chopped pecans
2 tablespoons minced green
  pepper
8 ounces cream cheese
½ cup sour cream
2 tablespoons milk
⅛ teaspoon white pepper

Tutti Frutti Sauce

You can serve this sauce hot or cold.
If you use candied citron, eliminate 1 tablespoon of sugar from the recipe.

Yields about 2½ cups

Cooking time: 2–4 hours
Preparation time: 30 minutes
Attention: Minimal
Pot size: 3–5 quarts

1 cup pineapple juice
¼ cup sugar
¼ teaspoon salt
1 cup pitted or candied cherries
½ cup citron peel (fresh or candied)
½ cup blanched almonds
4 slices pineapple

1. Mix the pineapple juice, sugar, and salt in the slow cooker and heat on a low setting for 1 to 2 hours.

2. Cut the cherries into quarters. Finely cut the citron peel. Cut the almonds in half; mince the pineapple.

3. Add the fruit and the almonds to the syrup in the slow cooker.

4. Cover and heat 1–2 hours on a low setting.

Tangiers Orange Sauce

This is irresistible drizzled over slices of ham, or on ice cream, cakes, or
sweet rolls. Also, try it on some otherwise bland vegetables, especially carrots.

Yields about 2½ cups

Cooking time: 3–4 hours
Preparation time: 30 minutes
Attention: Minimal
Pot size: 3–5 quarts

1¼ cups sugar
2 tablespoons cornstarch
1 teaspoon salt
1 teaspoon cinnamon
20 cloves
Zest of ¼ orange
2 cups orange juice
1 orange

1. Mix the sugar, starch, salt, spices, and orange zest in the slow cooker.

2. Stir in the orange juice. Cover and heat on a low setting for 2 to 3 hours.

3. Stir occasionally.

4. Slice the whole orange in cross sections. Half an hour before serving, add the orange slices to the slow cooker.

Wild Vanilla Sauce

*If you don't have fresh vanilla bean pods available,
you can use a teaspoon of vanilla extract instead.*

1. Mix the starch and sugar in the slow cooker, and then dissolve the starch mixture with the water.

2. Add the vanilla and salt. Cover and heat on a low setting for 2 to 3 hours.

3. An hour before serving, add the butter.

Yields about 3 cups

Cooking time: 3–4 hours
Preparation time: 30 minutes
Attention: Minimal
Pot size: 3–5 quarts

2 tablespoons cornstarch
1 cup sugar
2 cups water
1 4-inch vanilla bean pod
¼ teaspoon salt
¼ cup butter

Got-to-Have-It Chocolate Sauce

*This sauce keeps well in the refrigerator for weeks
(that is, if you can keep your spoon away from it).*

1. Combine the milk and powdered sugar in the slow cooker. Mince the chocolate; add the chocolate and the butter to the milk mixture.

2. Cover and heat on a low setting for 2 to 3 hours, stirring once or twice to mix.

Yields about 3 cups

Cooking time: 2–3 hours
Preparation time: 15 minutes
Attention: Minimal
Pot size: 3–5 quarts

1¼ cups evaporated milk
5½ cups powdered sugar
8 squares unsweetened
*   chocolate*
½ cup butter

Red County Barbecue Sauce

This sauce stores well, so take advantage.
Make some extra and refrigerate or freeze it, to reheat later as needed.

Yields about 4 cups

Cooking time: 3–4 hours
Preparation time: 15 minutes
Attention: Minimal
Pot size: 3–5 quarts

2 yellow onions
¼ cup oil
6 tomatoes
1 cup catsup
1 teaspoon salt
1 teaspoon celery seed
¼ cup brown sugar
¼ cup Worcestershire sauce
½ cup vinegar

1. Coarsely chop the onions. Sauté the onions in oil in a pan over medium heat until browned.

2. Cube the tomatoes. Combine the tomatoes and onions with the other ingredients in the slow cooker.

3. Cover and heat on a low setting for 3 to 4 hours.

Vodka Tomato Sauce

This goes well with angel hair pasta, garnished with fresh shavings of
Romano cheese and bright green asparagus tips or baby peas.

Yields 6–7 cups

Cooking time: 3–4 hours
Preparation time: 30 minutes
Attention: Minimum
Pot size: 3–5 quarts

2 onions
½ cup butter
1 cup vodka
12 tomatoes
2 cups heavy cream

1. Mince the onions. Sauté in butter in a pan over low heat until lightly browned. Stir in the vodka and transfer to the slow cooker.

2. Coarsely chop the tomatoes. Add to the slow cooker.

3. Cover and heat on a low setting for 2 to 3 hours.

4. Half an hour before serving, stir in the cream.

Smoky Barbecue Sauce

*Marjoram and liquid smoke can be found in the
spice sections of most grocery stores.
Marjoram is also available fresh in some stores, in the produce section.*

Yields about 2½ cups

Cooking time: 3–4 hours
Preparation time: 30 minutes
Attention: Minimal
Pot size: 3–5 quarts

1. Crush and slice the garlic; finely chop the onions. Sauté the garlic and onions in oil in a pan over low heat until soft.

2. Add the garlic and onions, tomato paste, salt, spices, sauces, liquid smoke, vinegar, wine, and water to the slow cooker.

3. Cover and heat on a low setting for 2 to 3 hours.

2 cloves garlic
2 onions
¼ cup oil
½ cup tomato paste
½ teaspoon salt
¼ teaspoon dry mustard
¼ teaspoon ginger
¼ teaspoon marjoram
¼ teaspoon seasoning salt
½ teaspoon rosemary
½ teaspoon oregano
1 tablespoon Worcestershire
    sauce
¼ teaspoon soy sauce
½ teaspoon A.1. sauce
¼ teaspoon Tabasco sauce
¼ teaspoon liquid smoke
½ cup vinegar
1 cup red wine
½ cup water

Slow Cooker Surprise

Maintain some suspense during your party. Keep some slow cookers sealed until a certain time of the evening. This way, desserts can be kept secret until it's time to serve them and dinner aromas will not be muddled by the scents of warm desserts.

Regal Caper Sauce

Yields about 3 cups

Cooking time: 2–3 hours
Preparation time: 30 minutes
Attention: Moderate
Pot size: 3–5 quarts

2 tablespoons butter
2 tablespoons flour
3 cups stock
½ teaspoon salt
½ teaspoon black
    peppercorns
1 egg yolk
1 tablespoon butter
6 tablespoons capers

This savory sauce is excellent on Royal Meatballs (page 22),
rabbit, fish, or other delicately flavored meats.
Use the stock that corresponds with the meat you choose.

1. Melt the butter in a saucepan over medium heat and mix in the flour, stirring until the flour is well mixed and slightly browned. Add one cup of the stock and mix well, then transfer to the slow cooker.

2. Add salt and peppercorns. Cover and heat on a low setting for 1 to 2 hours.

3. Half an hour before serving, skim with a strainer. Stir in the yolk and butter, then add the capers.

Olive Sherry Sauce

Yields about 3 cups

Cooking time: 1–2 hours
Preparation time: 60 minutes
Attention: Minimal
Pot size: 3–5 quarts

1 cup olives
1 cup dry sherry
2 cups brown or white gravy
¼ teaspoon salt
¼ teaspoon cayenne pepper

This sauce is best with Turkish or other dark, salty olives.
Try it drizzled over roast beef on thick slices of olive bread.

1. Pit and halve the olives. Heat the olive pieces in a saucepan with the sherry over low heat until most of the liquid has been absorbed.

2. Transfer the olives and thickened liquid to the slow cooker. Pour the gravy into the saucepan to incorporate any remaining olive liquid, then transfer it to the slow cooker. Add the salt and cayenne pepper.

3. Cover and heat on a low setting for 1 to 2 hours.

chapter 4
breads and grains

Parsley Almond Rice

This rice dish goes great with beef, chicken, curry, or seafood.
Use converted rice, not instant rice, for the best results.

Serves 6

Cooking time: 5–7 hours
Preparation time: 30 minutes
Attention: Minimal
Pot size: 3–5 quarts

*1 cup uncooked converted
    rice*
2 cups water
2 teaspoons salt
1 tablespoon butter
2 cloves garlic
¼ cup raw almonds
2 tablespoons butter
½ cup parsley

1. Put the rice, water, salt, and 1 tablespoon of butter in the slow cooker.

2. Cover and heat on a low setting for 4 to 6 hours.

3. Crush or mince the garlic and slice the almonds. Sauté the garlic and almonds in 2 tablespoons of butter in a pan over medium heat. Chop the parsley.

4. Half an hour before serving, stir the parsley into the almond mixture, then add to the rice.

Steamy Polenta

You can vary this recipe by adding sweetness with raisins or fruit, or savory flavors such as mushrooms, cheese, or herbs.

Makes about 5 cups

Cooking time: 2–3 hours
Preparation time: 15 minutes
Attention: Minimal
Pot size: 3–5 quarts

3¾ cups chicken stock
1 teaspoon salt
¼ teaspoon black pepper
1¼ cups cornmeal
1 tablespoon butter

1. Heat stock, salt, and pepper to a boil in a saucepan over medium heat. Add the cornmeal while stirring.

2. Grease a baking dish using 1 tablespoon butter and place the dish on a trivet in the slow cooker. Transfer the cornmeal mixture to the baking dish.

3. Cover the dish with foil or a ceramic or glass lid and pour water around the base of the trivet. Cover and heat on a low setting for 2 to 3 hours.

Give Lettuce a Second Life
Don't throw out that leftover salad. It will soon wilt if you already have dressing on it, so chop it up and throw it in the slow cooker with a vegetable dish of some type to cook overnight.

Classic Brown Bread

This old-fashioned bread is dense and sweet. Slow cooking is the only way to bring out the rich, caramelized flavors of the grains.

Yields 3 loaves

Cooking time: 3–4 hours
Preparation time: 45 minutes
Attention: Minimal
Pot size: 3–5 quarts

1 pound rye flour
1 pound graham flour
2 pounds cornmeal
1 pound wheat flour
3 teaspoons baking powder
1 quart molasses
1½ quarts milk
2 teaspoons salt
2 cups water

1. Sift the flour and baking powder together in a mixing bowl.

2. Mix the molasses, milk, and salt in a second mixing bowl. Add the milk mixture to the flour mixture to form a soft dough.

3. Grease and flour 3 loaf pans. Fill the pans one-half to three-quarters full; loosely cover each pan with foil or a glass or ceramic lid. Arrange the pans on a trivet or rack in the slow cooker, and pour 2 cups water around the base of the trivet.

4. Cover and heat on a high setting for 3 to 4 hours.

Shapely Sandwiches
Use cookie cutters to give your sandwiches fun and festive shapes. Cut the bread before adding sandwich toppings, or use the fun bread shapes in your breadbaskets. Also, use different types of bread for a colorful, as well as shapely effect.

Family Date Bread

Try this toasted with butter or honey.
Or cream butter with honey and serve the mixture as a spread for the bread.

1. Chop the dates. Boil the water and pour it over the dates; let stand.

2. Cream the butter and sugar. Add the vanilla, egg, and salt to the butter mixture. Add the cooled dates, and the water they're sitting in, to the egg mixture. Fold in the raisins and nuts.

3. Sift the flour, baking soda, and baking powder together in a bowl. Add the egg mixture to the flour mixture.

4. Grease and flour 3 loaf pans, or the equivalent. Fill the pans one-half to three-quarters full; loosely cover each pan with foil or a glass or ceramic lid. Arrange the pans on a trivet or rack in the slow cooker, and pour water around the base of the trivet.

5. Cover and heat on a high setting for 2 to 3 hours.

Yields 3 loaves

Cooking time: 2–3 hours
Preparation time: 45 minutes
Attention: Minimal
Pot size: 3–5 quarts

8 ounces dried dates
1½ cups water
4 tablespoons butter
2 cups sugar
½ teaspoon vanilla
1 egg
½ teaspoon salt
1 cup raisins
1 cup nuts
4 cups flour
2 teaspoons baking soda
4 teaspoons baking powder

Pineapple Banana Bread

*This is nice to serve at parties in the winter,
when everyone wants to be on a tropical island instead of shoveling snow.*

Yields 2 loaves

Cooking time: 2–3 hours
Preparation time: 30 minutes
Attention: Minimal
Pot size: 3–5 quarts

3 cups flour
2 cups sugar
½ teaspoon baking soda
1½ teaspoons baking powder
3 eggs
½ pound pineapple
1½ cups oil
½ teaspoon salt
2 cups bananas

1. Combine and mix the flour, sugar, baking soda, and baking powder well.

2. Beat the eggs in a separate bowl. Crush or dice the pineapple. If the pineapple is canned, include the juice; otherwise, supplement with ¼ cup water or fruit juice.

3. Mix the eggs, pineapple, oil, salt, and bananas, and then add to the dry ingredients.

4. Grease and flour 2 loaf pans. Fill the pans one-half to three-quarters full; loosely cover each pan with foil or a glass or ceramic lid. Arrange the pans on a trivet or rack in the slow cooker, and pour water around the base of the trivet.

5. Cover and heat on a high setting for 2 to 3 hours.

Easy Accessories

Get the most use out of your slow cooker. Collect muffin tins, bread pans, and custard glasses small enough to fit in your brand and size of slow cooker. These can be metal, glass, or ceramic. Anything ovenproof will work.

Fresh Apple Bread

You'll be amazed at the range of tastes different apple varieties take on after baking. Try this recipe with different types of apples for a change of flavor.

Yields 1 loaf

Cooking time: 2–3 hours
Preparation time: 45 minutes
Attention: Minimal
Pot size: 3–5 quarts

1 cup sugar
½ cup shortening
2 eggs
1½ teaspoons vanilla
1½ tablespoons buttermilk
½ teaspoon salt
1½ cups peeled and minced
*   apples*
1 cup pecans
2 cups flour
1 teaspoon baking soda
1 teaspoon cinnamon
3 tablespoons sugar

1. Cream the first cup of sugar with the shortening.

2. Beat the eggs. Add the eggs, vanilla, buttermilk, and salt to the creamed ingredients. Fold the minced apples and pecans into the liquid mixture.

3. Sift the flour and baking soda together. Add the liquid mixture to the sifted mixture.

4. Grease and flour 1 loaf pan, or the equivalent. Fill the baking dish one-half to three-quarters full. Sprinkle the batter with the cinnamon and sugar. Loosely cover with foil or a glass or ceramic lid to prevent condensation from falling in. Arrange the dish on a trivet or rack in the slow cooker, and pour water around the base of the trivet.

5. Cover and heat on a high setting for 2 to 3 hours.

Cheap Goods

Instead of a knife, use taut dental floss to slice cakes and breads. Just be sure you don't use flavored or heavily waxed floss. The great thing is, you don't even have to wash up afterward—just throw the used floss away!

Holiday Gift Cake

Cooking time: 2–3 hours
Preparation time: 45 minutes
Attention: Minimal
Pot size: 3–5 quarts

2 cups mayonnaise
2 cups sugar
2 cups water
2 teaspoons vanilla
1½ cups walnuts
½ pound dried or candied
    fruits
1 cup raisins
3 ounces candied cherries
½ pound dates
3 ounces candied pineapple
4 cups flour
2 teaspoons baking soda
2 teaspoons cinnamon
2 teaspoons nutmeg

*A cake with mayonnaise in it? Your guests might be wary of this ingredient,
so don't reveal it until they've tasted it and asked for a second slice.*

1. Cream the mayonnaise and sugar; then add the water and vanilla. Chop the nuts and dried fruits; then stir into the mayonnaise mixture.

2. Sift the flour with the baking soda; then stir in the spices.

3. Add the flour mixture to the mayonnaise mixture.

4. Grease and flour 3 loaf pans, or the equivalent. Fill the baking dishes one-half to three-quarters full; loosely cover each dish with foil or a glass or ceramic lid. Arrange the dishes on a trivet or rack in the slow cooker, and pour water around the base of the trivet.

5. Cover and heat on a high setting for 2 to 3 hours.

Sifting Flour

Flour settles and packs as it sits. So, before measuring any flour, sift it to loosen the flour particles. Otherwise your dishes may not come out as they should, and may be different each time you prepare them.

Orange Raisin Bread

This bread goes well with wild game. The citrus flavor is an especially nice complement to duck and goose, lightening the richness of the meat.

Yields 1 loaf

Cooking time: 2–3 hours
Preparation time: 45 minutes
Attention: Minimal
Pot size: 3–5 quarts

1 orange
¾ cup raisins
½ cup water
2 tablespoons butter
1 cup sugar
1 teaspoon baking soda
1 teaspoon vanilla
2 cups flour
1 teaspoon baking powder
⅛ teaspoon salt
1 egg

1. Grate the orange peel. Extract the juice from the orange, reserve; discard the remaining flesh. Mix the grated peel with the raisins and grind or finely mince together.

2. Boil the water and add it to the juice; add this to the peel-and-raisin mixture. Add the butter, sugar, baking soda, and vanilla to this; then let this orange mixture cool.

3. Sift the flour, baking powder, and salt together. Beat the egg and add it to the cooled orange mixture; then add the flour mixture to the orange-and-egg mixture.

4. Grease and flour 1 loaf pan or the equivalent. Fill the baking dish one-half to three-quarters full; loosely cover the dish with foil or a glass or ceramic lid. Arrange the dish on a trivet or rack in the slow cooker, and pour water around the base of the trivet.

5. Cover and heat on a high setting for 2 to 3 hours.

Pecan Rhubarb Bread

Yields 2 loaves

Cooking time: 2–3 hours
Preparation time: 45 minutes
Attention: Minimal
Pot size: 3–5 quarts

1½ cups diced rhubarb
½ cup chopped pecans
1½ cups brown sugar
⅔ cup salad oil
1 egg
1 cup sour milk
1 teaspoon salt
1 teaspoon baking soda
1 teaspoon vanilla
2½ cups flour
½ cup sugar mixed with
*   1 tablespoon butter*

To make sour milk, add 1 tablespoon white vinegar or lemon juice to enough fresh milk to make a total of 1 cup. Let it stand for 15 minutes before using.

1. Mix all the ingredients (except sugar–butter mixture) in the order listed.

2. Grease and flour 2 loaf pans or the equivalent. Fill the baking dishes one-half to three-quarters full.

3. Sprinkle the batter with the sugar–butter blend.

4. Loosely cover each dish with foil or a glass or ceramic lid. Arrange the dishes on a trivet or rack in the slow cooker, and pour water around the base of the trivet.

5. Cover and heat on a high setting for 2 to 3 hours.

Using Muffin Tins

If you find that your steamed apples, tomatoes, or peppers become misshapen during cooking, use this handy trick. Steam these items in muffin tins to help them keep their shape. If the pans aren't nonstick, butter or oil them before use.

Chocolaty Banana Bread

Did you ever eat "Monkey Tails" in Disneyland? They're frozen bananas dipped in chocolate. You'll find that same taste in this bread.

1. Cream the butter, sugar, and eggs. Mash the bananas, and add to the creamed mix.

2. Sift together the flour, salt, and baking soda, then add to the liquid ingredients. Fold in the nuts, chocolate, and cherries.

3. Grease and flour 3 loaf pans or the equivalent. Fill the baking dishes one-half to three-quarters full; loosely cover each dish with foil or a glass or ceramic lid. Arrange the dishes on a trivet or rack in the slow cooker, and pour water around the base of the trivet.

4. Cover and heat on a high setting for 2 to 3 hours.

Cooling Slow-Cooked Bread
When making bread in the slow cooker, you can let the loaves cool in their baking containers before removing them for slicing. Take them out of the slow cooker, and leave them on a rack until they're cool to the touch.

Yields 3 loaves

Cooking time: 2–3 hours
Preparation time: 45 minutes
Attention: Minimal
Pot size: 3–5 quarts

1 cup butter
2 cups sugar
4 eggs
2 cups bananas
4 cups flour
1 teaspoon salt
2 teaspoons baking soda
½ cup nutmeats of choice
½ cup chocolate chips
1 cup maraschino cherries

Cherry Date Brown Bread

This bread is perfect for dipping in Brandied Chocolate Fondue (page 43).
It freezes well, too.

Yields 3 loaves

Cooking time: 2–3 hours
Preparation time: 45 minutes
Attention: Minimal
Pot size: 3–5 quarts

1 cup dried dates, pitted
1 cup dried cherries, pitted
2 teaspoons baking soda
2 cups water
2 cups brown sugar
2 tablespoons shortening
2 eggs
1 teaspoon vanilla
1 teaspoon salt
2 cups white flour
2 cups whole wheat flour
½ cup nutmeats of choice

1. Chop the dates. Mix the dates, cherries, and baking soda; boil the water, add it to the date mixture, and let it steep.

2. While the date mixture is cooling, cream the sugar and shortening. Beat the eggs; add to the creamed ingredients. After cooling, add liquids not absorbed by the date mixture.

3. Add the remaining ingredients to the egg mixture in the order given, folding in the nuts and the steeped fruit last.

4. Grease and flour 3 loaf pans or the equivalent. Fill the baking dishes half full; loosely cover each dish with foil or a glass or ceramic lid. Arrange the dishes on a trivet or rack in the slow cooker, and pour water around the base of the trivet.

5. Cover and heat on a high setting for 2 to 3 hours.

Cakes for Dipping

When choosing cake to dip in your sauces, you have a variety of options. Virtually any cake—from pound cake to angel food—will work. Stale cake is even better; it is dry enough to soak up sauce without crumbling.

Pumpkin Pie Bread

Pumpkin is a wonderful flavor year-round, not just during the holidays. This bread goes well with poultry, and it freezes well.

1. Sift the flour and baking soda, then add the salt and spices.

2. Beat the eggs and blend with the pumpkin, sugar, oil, and vanilla. Add the liquid mix to the dry ingredients and mix well.

3. Grease and flour 2 loaf pans or the equivalent. Fill the baking dishes one-half to three-quarters full; loosely cover each dish with foil or a glass or ceramic lid. Arrange the dishes on a trivet or rack in the slow cooker, and pour water around the base of the trivet.

4. Cover and heat on a high setting for 2 to 3 hours.

Yields 2 loaves

Cooking time: 2–3 hours
Preparation time: 30 minutes
Attention: Minimal
Pot size: 3–5 quarts

3½ cups flour
2 teaspoons baking soda
1½ teaspoons salt
1 teaspoon nutmeg
1 teaspoon cinnamon
⅛ teaspoon mace
4 eggs
2 cups cooked pumpkin
3 cups sugar
1 cup oil
1 teaspoon vanilla

Tropical Bread

*This pineapple-and-coconut-flavored bread goes well
with curry dishes like Chicken Mulligatawny Soup (page 170)
and Rajah's Apple Curry Soup (page 72).*

Yields 3 loaves

Cooking time: 2–3 hours
Preparation time: 30 minutes
Attention: Minimal
Pot size: 3–5 quarts

3½ cups pineapple
1½ cups sugar
2 teaspoons salt
2 teaspoons baking soda
4 eggs
10 ounces flaked coconut
4 cups flour

1. Crush or shred the pineapple. If using canned pineapple, include the juice. If fresh, add water or fruit juice to cover the fruit.

2. Add the sugar, salt, and baking soda to the fruit. Beat the eggs well and stir into the fruit mixture, then fold in the coconut.

3. Add the liquid mixture to the flour.

4. Grease and flour 3 loaf pans or the equivalent. Fill the baking dishes one-half to three-quarters full; loosely cover each dish with foil or a glass or ceramic lid. Arrange the dishes on a trivet or rack in the slow cooker, and pour water around the base of the trivet.

5. Cover and heat on a high setting for 2 to 3 hours.

Make-Your-Own Bread Tins
So, you thought you couldn't make bread in a slow cooker? You don't even need to buy more pans. Use clean soup cans, coffee cans, or Pyrex bowls. Give each a little lid of aluminum foil, a glass saucer, or an inverted Pyrex bowl to keep out condensation.

Cinnamon Orange Oat Bread

You can also make this with lemonade instead of orange juice.
Just be sure it's lemonade; straight lemon juice would be too tart.

1. Sift the flour, baking powder, and baking soda together. Stir in the sugar, salt, cinnamon, raisins, and oats.

2. Beat the egg; mix it with the shortening, orange juice, and water. Add to the dry mixture and mix well.

3. Grease and flour 1 loaf pan or the equivalent. Fill the baking dish one-half to three-quarters full and sprinkle with ¼ cup raisins.

4. Loosely cover the dish with foil or a glass or ceramic lid. Arrange the dish on a trivet or rack in the slow cooker, and pour water around the base of the trivet.

5. Cover and heat on a high setting for 2 to 3 hours.

Handling Baking Tins
How do you get your slow-cooked bread out of those round cans? With a can opener! Just wait until the can has cooled, open the bottom, and push out your round loaf. Just watch out for sharp edges when handling the cans.

Cooking time: 2–3 hours
Preparation time: 45 minutes
Attention: Minimal
Pot size: 3–5 quarts

1½ cups flour
2 teaspoons baking powder
½ teaspoon baking soda
½ cup sugar
½ teaspoon salt
1 teaspoon cinnamon
¾ cup raisins
1 cup uncooked oats
1 egg
2 tablespoons shortening
½ cup orange juice
½ cup water
¼ cup raisins

Hot Daybreak Cereal

You can either buy multigrain cereal or mix your own from rolled oats, crunchy breakfast cereals (like granola), and cracked wheat.

Serves 4

Cooking time: 6–8 hours
Preparation time: 15 minutes
Attention: Minimal
Pot size: 3–5 quarts

2 apples
1 cup multigrain cereal
¼ teaspoon salt
4 cups water

1. Core and slice the apples. Mix the apples, cereal, salt, and water in the slow cooker.

2. Cover and heat on a low setting for 6 to 8 hours.

Cooking Dried Beans and Grains

There's a rule of thumb for cooking dried beans and grains in a slow cooker: Use two volumes of water for each volume of dried material. If you open the lid and it's still not enough, just add more and keep cooking.

Farmhouse Oats

This is the original hot cereal for cold mornings.
Top with your choice of fresh fruit, brown sugar, and cold milk.

Serves 4

Cooking time: 6–8 hours
Preparation time: 15 minutes
Attention: Minimal
Pot size: 3–5 quarts

1¼ cups steel-cut oats
½ teaspoon salt
4 cups water

1. Mix the oats, salt, and water in the slow cooker.

2. Cover and heat on a low setting for 6 to 8 hours.

Tangy Rice

This is a nice change from plain rice.
The tart-and-tangy flavor is especially suitable as a side dish for wild game.

1. Cut the bacon into 1-inch pieces and sauté in a pan over medium heat until browned.

2. Add the shortening and let it melt, then transfer the bacon and fat to the slow cooker.

3. Mince the onion. Add the onion, rice, sauerkraut, and pepper to the slow cooker. Mix the ingredients well, then add the water and stir again.

4. Cover and heat on a low setting for 4 to 6 hours.

Serves 8

Cooking time: 4–6 hours
Preparation time: 30 minutes
Attention: Minimal
Pot size: 3–5 quarts

6 slices bacon
1 tablespoon shortening
1 onion
1½ cups uncooked converted rice
4 cups sauerkraut
¼ teaspoon freshly ground black pepper
4 cups water

Savory Rye Berries

Cooking time: 6–8 hours
Preparation time: 30 minutes
Attention: Minimal
Pot size: 3–5 quarts

1 onion
3 tablespoons butter
1 cup rye berries
2 cups water
1 teaspoon salt

*Whole grains of rye and wheat are called "berries,"
just as whole grains of corn are called "kernels."*

1. Chop the onion; sauté in butter in a pan over medium heat until soft.

2. Put the rye, water, salt, and onion in the slow cooker.

3. Cover and heat on a low setting for 6 to 8 hours.

Beyond Rice

Move on from white rice. Take advantage of the power of slow cooking and start cooking unbroken grains, called "berries," which take longer to cook. Berries yield an entirely different taste, nutty and chewy. Try rye berries, wheat berries, or barley. Use 1 cup berries with 2 cups water, and cook for about 8 hours on low.

chapter 5
soups and stews

Corn and Dumpling Soup

Serves 12

Cooking time: 4–5 hours
Preparation time: 30 minutes
Attention: Minimal
Pot size: 3–5 quarts

1 clove garlic
3 carrots
1 onion
4 stalks celery
2 potatoes
6 cups beef stock
1 teaspoon salt
10 saltine crackers
½ pound ground beef
¼ pound ground smoked ham
1 egg
¼ teaspoon salt
1 tablespoon oil
3 cups cream-style corn
1 tablespoon finely minced
    parsley

*You can substitute ground turkey for the beef and ham in these dumplings,
and switch to a chicken stock instead of beef stock.*

1. Sliver the garlic; finely slice the carrots, onion, celery, and potatoes.

2. In the slow cooker, mix the garlic, cut vegetables, stock, and 1 teaspoon salt. Cover and heat on a low setting for 3 to 4 hours.

3. Finely crumble the crackers. Mix the cracker crumbs, beef, ham, egg, and ¼ teaspoon salt. Form the mixture into small balls about ¾ inch in size.

4. Sauté the meatballs in oil in a pan over high heat until browned; drain.

5. An hour before serving, add the meatballs, corn, and parsley to the slow cooker.

Lentil Soup

To give the soup more body, mash or puree some of the cooked lentils in your blender or food processor and add before serving.

1. Soak the lentils in cold water in the slow cooker for 6 hours; drain and discard the water. Place the lentils back in the slow cooker.

2. Chop the onions. Sauté the onions in butter in a pan over medium heat until soft. Transfer to the slow cooker.

3. Slice the carrots diagonally. Combine the carrots, broth, bone, salt, and bouquet garni with the other ingredients in the slow cooker.

4. Cover and heat on a low setting for 4 to 5 hours.

5. Before serving, remove the bouquet garni.

Serves 6

Cooking time: 3–4 hours
Preparation time: 30 minutes
Attention: Minimal
Pot size: 3–5 quarts

2 pounds brown lentils
2 yellow onions
2 tablespoons butter
2 carrots
4 cups chicken broth
1 ham bone
¼ teaspoon salt
1 bouquet garni

Soup of Tomorrow

Turn the cold leftovers of today into a hot Soup of Tomorrow!
You can even use your leftover salad, with or without dressing.

Serves 6

Cooking time: 3–4 hours
Preparation time: 30 minutes
Attention: Minimal
Pot size: 3–5 quarts

1 medium onion
2 tablespoons butter
2 tablespoons flour
1–2 cups leftover green salad
2 cups leftover cooked
vegetables
2 cups liquid left over from
cooking meat
¼ teaspoon salt
¼ teaspoon pepper
2 cups milk

1. Finely chop the onion. Sauté the onion in butter in a pan over low heat until the onion is soft. Stir in flour until well blended.

2. Chop the salad and vegetables. Combine the onion, salad, vegetables, cooking broth, and salt and pepper in the slow cooker.

3. Cover and heat on a low setting for 2 to 3 hours.

4. An hour before serving, stir in the milk.

Rajah's Apple Curry Soup

Curry is actually a mixture of other spices, which may include turmeric, cardamom, or coriander. Try using different commercial curries to see the difference.

Serves 12

Cooking time: 5–6 hours
Preparation time: 30 minutes
Attention: Minimal
Pot size: 3–5 quarts

3 pounds fresh mushrooms
2 tablespoons olive oil
5 tablespoons flour
½ cup dried mushrooms
3 medium tart apples, peeled
7½ cups chicken broth
1½ teaspoons turmeric
2¼ teaspoons ground ginger
2¼ teaspoons ground cumin
2¼ teaspoons curry powder
¾ teaspoon ground coriander
1 cup sherry
¾ cup heavy cream

1. Slice the fresh mushrooms and heat in olive oil in a pan over medium heat until soft, then blend in the flour.

2. Slice the dried mushrooms into strips; coarsely chop the apples.

3. Combine the sautéed and dried mushrooms, apples, broth, and spices in the slow cooker.

4. Cover and heat on a low setting for 4 to 5 hours.

5. Half an hour before serving, add the sherry and the cream.

Chef Jeff's Chili

Try substituting other types of beans,
like pinto, black, or butter beans, for a different flavor.

Serves 8

Cooking time: 4–5 hours
Preparation time: 30 minutes
Attention: Minimal
Pot size: 3–5 quarts

2 pounds ground beef
1 onion
2 cloves garlic
3 stalks celery
2 pounds tomatoes
1 bell pepper
2 pounds cooked kidney
    beans
1 cup tomato paste
2 tablespoons chili powder
1 teaspoon basil
1 teaspoon pepper
2 bay leaves
1 teaspoon salt

1. Sauté the beef in a pan over medium heat until brown, then drain, reserving ½ cup of the fat and juices. Transfer the meat to the slow cooker.

2. Coarsely chop the onion, garlic, and celery. Sauté in the pan with the meat fat and juices over medium heat until soft. Transfer the onion mixture to the slow cooker.

3. Dice the tomatoes and bell pepper. Add the tomatoes, bell pepper, beans, tomato paste, spices, and salt to the slow cooker.

4. Cover and heat on a low setting for 4 to 5 hours. Before serving, remove the bay leaves.

Have a Cook-Off

Have your own chili cook-off. Choose five or six chili recipes and make them all. Let your guests choose the winner, sampling small bowls from each slow cooker. Or have your guests bring their own chili recipes to see how they compare. Either way, there will be lots of yummy leftovers for everyone.

Rich Sausage and Cabbage Soup

*Serve this with slices of warm wheat bread, thick enough to dunk,
or thin enough to use for small sausage sandwiches.*

Serves 8

Cooking time: 5–6 hours
Preparation time: 30 minutes
Attention: Minimal
Pot size: 3–5 quarts

¼ pound prosciutto
½ pound spicy sausage
2 tablespoons olive oil
2 onions
3 cloves garlic
1 pound turnips
½ head green cabbage
6 dried tomatoes
2 pounds cooked butter
   beans
6 cups chicken broth
4 cups loose spinach leaves
¾ cup dry sherry

1. Chop the prosciutto and sausage into ¼-inch pieces. Sauté the prosciutto and sausage in olive oil in a pan over medium heat until browned. Transfer the meat to the slow cooker, leaving the fat and juices in the pan.

2. Coarsely chop the onions and mince the garlic. Sauté the onions and garlic in the pan with the meat juices until soft. Transfer to the slow cooker.

3. Peel and cube the turnips. Cut the cabbage into 1-inch segments. Cut the dried tomatoes into ¼-inch strips. Drain the butter beans. Transfer the cut vegetables and beans to the slow cooker.

4. Add the chicken broth to the slow cooker. Cover and heat on a low setting for 4 to 5 hours.

5. Cut the spinach into ½-inch strips. Add the spinach and the sherry half an hour before serving.

Thicken Things Up

If your gravy, sauce, or soup is too thin, add a dash of instant mashed potato flakes. Depending on the dish, other options are to add some instant grits or oatmeal, or even tapioca.

Roasted Red Pepper Soup

If you have a grill, try preparing your own sweet red peppers.
Cut 3 peppers, brush with oil, and grill until tender.

1. Chop the onion and sauté in oil in a pan over medium heat until soft, then stir in the flour. Add mixture to the slow cooker.

2. Drain and chop the red bell peppers. Combine with the sugar, broth, salt, and pepper in the slow cooker.

3. Cover and heat on a low setting for 2 to 3 hours.

4. Use a slotted spoon to remove some of the onion and peppers. Puree them in a food processor and return them to the slow cooker.

5. Half an hour before serving, stir in the sherry and cream.

Serves 4

Cooking time: 3–4 hours
Preparation time: 30 minutes
Attention: Moderate
Pot size: 3–5 quarts

1 onion
1 tablespoon vegetable oil
1 tablespoon flour
2 7½-ounce jars roasted red
*   bell peppers*
1 teaspoon sugar
3½ cups broth
½ teaspoon salt
½ teaspoon black pepper
2 tablespoons dry sherry
¼ cup heavy cream

Leek and Potato Soup

Leeks are mild in soup. Therefore, this soup is excellent before
strongly flavored main dishes of beef or wild game.

1. Thinly slice the leeks and onion. Sauté the leeks and onion in butter in a pan over low heat until soft. Transfer to the slow cooker.

2. Cube the potatoes. Combine with the stock, water, salt, pepper, and bouquet garni in the slow cooker.

3. Cover and heat on a low setting for 4 to 5 hours.

4. Coarsely chop the parsley. Before serving, remove the bouquet garni and stir the parsley into the soup.

Serves 6

Cooking time: 4–5 hours
Preparation time: 30 minutes
Attention: Minimal
Pot size: 3–5 quarts

4 leeks
1 onion
3 tablespoons butter
2 pounds potatoes
4 cups beef or chicken stock
2 cups water
½ teaspoon salt
½ teaspoon black pepper
1 bouquet garni
1 bunch parsley

Red and Yellow Vegetable Soup

*Time the preparation of this soup so you can serve it freshly cooked,
with freshly chopped red peppers as a garnish.*

Serves 8

Cooking time: 3–4 hours
Preparation time: 30 minutes
Attention: Moderate
Pot size: 3–5 quarts

3 cloves garlic
3 leeks
2 tablespoons olive oil
1 potato
1 yellow squash
2 red bell peppers
8 green onions
4½ cups chicken broth
2 cups corn kernels
1½ teaspoons dried tarragon
1 teaspoon ground cumin
½ teaspoon salt
1 cup corn kernels

1. Crush and coarsely chop the garlic. Thinly slice the leeks, the white part only. Sauté the garlic and leeks in the olive oil in a pan over low heat until soft. Add to slow cooker.

2. Cube the potato and finely slice the squash. Transfer to the slow cooker.

3. Mince the bell peppers and green onions. Set aside one-fourth of the peppers and onions uncooked. Transfer the rest to the slow cooker.

4. Add the broth, 1 cup of corn, spices, and salt to the slow cooker. Cover and heat on a low setting for 2 to 3 hours.

5. Before serving, use a slotted spoon to remove some of the vegetables. Puree them in a blender or food processor and return them to the slow cooker. Stir in the uncooked minced bell peppers and green onions and the last cup of corn.

Converting Recipes
Wouldn't you like to convert your own secret recipes to be made with your slow cooker? You can! One hour of conventional cooking at 350°F is about the same as eight hours of slow cooking on a low setting, or four hours on a high setting.

Lentil and Barley Soup

*As with all soup bones, ask your butcher for some bones
that have some meat remaining. This adds flavor and nutrients.*

1. Coarsely chop the onion and mince the garlic.

2. Combine the onion, garlic, bones, water, salt, and spices in the slow cooker.

3. Rinse the lentils and remove any stones. Add the lentils and barley to the slow cooker.

4. Cover and heat on a low setting for 4 to 5 hours.

5. Coarsely chop the parsley and provide as a garnish for individual servings. Remove the bay leaves before serving.

A Garlic Project

*Some evening while you're sitting at home talking on the phone or
watching television, peel a dozen or so cloves of garlic and put them in
a small jar of olive or vegetable oil. This will keep the garlic fresh and
give the oil a nice flavor for future use in recipes or salad dressings.*

Serves 8

Cooking time: 3–4 hours
Preparation time: 30 minutes
Attention: Minimal
Pot size: 3–5 quarts

1 onion
3 cloves garlic
1½ pounds lamb bones
8 cups water
½ teaspoon salt
2 bay leaves
¼ teaspoon black pepper
1 cup brown lentils
½ cup pearl barley
1 bunch fresh parsley

Serves 10

Cooking time: 3–4 hours
Preparation time: 30 minutes
Attention: Minimal
Pot size: 3–5 quarts

1 onion
2 leeks
2 stalks celery
1 bay leaf
1 clove
3 tablespoons butter
½ cup flour
8 cups milk
2 pounds potatoes
1 ham bone
½ teaspoon salt
⅛ teaspoon cayenne pepper
1 egg yolk
1 cup cream

Cream of Potato Soup

*This creamy soup is delicious with warm slices
of a dark bread like pumpernickel.*

1. Coarsely chop the onion and leeks. Cut the celery diagonally.

2. Sauté the onion, leeks, celery, bay leaf, and clove in butter in a pan over low heat until the onion is soft. Stir in the flour until it is mixed in well. Add 1 cup of the milk and mix well. Transfer to the slow cooker.

3. Slice the potatoes. Transfer to the slow cooker, along with the ham bone, salt, pepper, and remaining milk.

4. Cover and heat on a low setting for 2 to 3 hours.

5. Mix the yolk and cream. Half an hour before serving, stir in the yolk and cream mixture. Remove bay leaf before serving.

Yields about 4 cups

Cooking time: 2–3 hours
Preparation time: 15 minutes
Attention: Moderate
Pot size: 3–5 quarts

2 pounds chicken bones
4 cups water
1 bouquet garni
½ teaspoon salt

Chef's Chicken Broth

*If you bake a chicken or a turkey,
keep the carcass after you've removed the meat.
This can be used to make broth, which you can freeze and use for soup later.*

1. Put the carcass, with larger bones cracked, into the slow cooker with the water, bouquet garni, and salt.

2. Cover and heat on a low setting for 2 to 3 hours.

3. Before using, strain to remove the bones and bouquet garni.

Cream of Corn and Onion Soup

*If you don't have a corn grater,
carefully use a sharp knife to pare the fresh kernels off the cob.*

1. Mince the onions and remove the corn from the cob. Transfer the onions and corn to the slow cooker.

2. Melt the butter in a saucepan over medium heat and stir in the flour, mixing over medium heat until the flour becomes slightly browned. Stir in 1 cup of the chicken broth and transfer the flour mixture to the slow cooker.

3. Add the remaining broth, salt, and pepper to the slow cooker. Cover and heat on a low setting for 3 to 4 hours.

4. Half an hour before serving, add the cream.

Serves 6

Cooking time: 4–5 hours
Preparation time: 30 minutes
Attention: Minimal
Pot size: 3–5 quarts

6 onions
6 raw ears of corn
2 tablespoons butter
2 tablespoons flour
4 cups chicken broth
¼ teaspoon salt
½ teaspoon black pepper
1 cup cream

Pickelsteiner Three-Meat Stew

The original recipe calls for veal,
but the slow cooker will tenderize older cuts of beef just as well.

Serves 18

Cooking time: 6–8 hours
Preparation time: 30 minutes
Attention: Minimal
Pot size: 5 quarts

1 onion
2 pounds beef
2 pounds lamb
2 pounds pork
2 tablespoons butter
½ cup flour
2 pounds potatoes
2 cups tomato sauce
2 cups beef stock
¼ teaspoon salt
¼ teaspoon black pepper
1 bouquet garni

1. Mince the onion. Cut the meat into 1-inch cubes.

2. Sauté the meat and onion in butter in a pan over medium heat until browned. Stir in the flour until well mixed. Transfer to the slow cooker.

3. Cube the potatoes. Combine with the tomato sauce, stock, salt, pepper, and bouquet garni in the slow cooker.

4. Cover and heat on a low setting for 6 to 8 hours.

5. Before serving, remove the bouquet garni.

An Essential Tool

If you don't have one already, be sure to get an all-in-one apple corer and slicer. Use this simple tool to prepare apples, pears, potatoes, or turnips easily. These are fairly inexpensive and come in handy for almost any recipe.

Spring Soup

If you happen to have your own asparagus bed, you'll want to use this recipe more than once in the spring and early summer.

1. Peel and slice the carrots and turnips lengthwise into 2-inch strips. Cut the beans diagonally. Cut 2-inch tips from the asparagus and the florets from the cauliflower; set aside the asparagus stalks and cauliflower stems for use in other recipes.

2. Combine the cut vegetables with the peas, broth, salt, and pepper in the slow cooker.

3. Cover and heat on a low setting for 3 to 4 hours.

4. Chop the cilantro. Half an hour before serving, stir in the cilantro.

Serves 6

Cooking time: 4–5 hours
Preparation time: 30 minutes
Attention: Minimal
Pot size: 3–5 quarts

½ pound carrots
½ pound turnips
½ pound string beans
3 pounds fresh asparagus
1 pound cauliflower
1 cup green peas
2 cups chicken broth
¼ teaspoon salt
¼ teaspoon black pepper
½ cup cilantro

Old-Fashioned Onion Soup

*Make your own croutons to serve with this soup.
Cut thick slices of black bread into cubes.
Sprinkle with grated Parmesan and pepper, then broil until browned.*

1. Thinly slice the onions. Slowly sauté in butter in pan over low heat until browned.

2. Add onions, broth, salt, and peppercorns to the slow cooker.

3. Cover and heat on a low setting for 3 to 4 hours.

4. Grate the Parmesan. Before serving, stir ¼ cup grated cheese into the soup. Set out the remainder to garnish individual servings.

Serves 8

Cooking time: 3–4 hours
Preparation time: 30 minutes
Attention: Minimal
Pot size: 3–5 quarts

6 yellow onions
6 tablespoons butter
4 cups beef broth
½ teaspoon salt
½ teaspoon black
*   peppercorns*
¼ pound fresh Parmesan
*   cheese*

Very Onion Soup

This soup has not only onions, but also leeks, shallots, and scallions.
All become tender and sweet after slow cooking.

Serves 6

Cooking time: 4–5 hours
Preparation time: 30 minutes
Attention: Moderate
Pot size: 3–5 quarts

2 yellow onions
4 leeks
¼ pound shallots
6 cloves garlic
¼ cup butter
4 cups chicken stock
¼ teaspoon salt
1 teaspoon thyme
1 bay leaf
½ teaspoon pepper
3 scallions
1 cup heavy cream

1. Finely chop the onions. Thinly slice the leeks, the white parts only. Chop the shallots and mince the garlic.

2. Sauté the onions, leeks, shallots, and garlic in butter in a pan over low heat until the onion is lightly browned.

3. Put the onion mixture into the slow cooker. Add the stock, salt, and spices.

4. Cover and heat on a low setting for 3 to 4 hours.

5. Slice the scallions into ¼-inch pieces. Half an hour before serving, remove some of the onion mixture from the slow cooker with a slotted spoon and transfer to a blender or food processor. Puree with the cream and return to the slow cooker. Add the sliced scallions to the slow cooker.

Handy Tortillas

Soups and stews can be thickened by stirring in some dried, crumbled corn tortillas. The corn is nutritious and falls apart easily when wet. Use corn tortillas, not flour tortillas, which are more elastic.

White Bean Soup

You can substitute a ham bone for the bacon strips in this recipe, especially if the ham bone is a meaty one.

Serves 8

Cooking time: 8–10 hours
Preparation time: 30 minutes
Attention: Minimal
Pot size: 3–5 quarts

2 pounds white beans
6 strips bacon
2 potatoes
6 cups chicken broth
½ teaspoon black pepper
1 onion
1 carrot
1 stalk celery
3 tablespoons butter
2 tablespoons flour
½ cup parsley

1. Soak the beans in water overnight, then drain and discard the water.

2. Sauté the bacon in a pan over medium heat until crisp; drain. Crumble the bacon. Chop the potatoes. Combine the beans, bacon, potatoes, broth, and pepper in the slow cooker.

3. Cover and heat on a low setting for 8 to 10 hours.

4. Mince the onion, grate the carrot, and thinly slice the celery. Sauté the onion, carrot, and celery in butter in a pan over medium heat until the onion is browned, then stir in the flour until blended. Half an hour before serving, add the browned mixture to the slow cooker.

5. Coarsely chop the parsley. Before serving, stir the parsley into the soup.

Take It to the Bank

Keep a plastic tub labeled "Soup Bank" in your freezer. Whenever you have leftovers that are potential soup fixings, such as a piece of fried chicken, some vegetables, or a handful of fried rice, pop them in the soup bank. When you're ready, cash in and make soup.

Busy Day Beef Stew

Serves 6

Cooking time: 4–5 hours
Preparation time: 30 minutes
Attention: Minimal
Pot size: 3–5 quarts

2 pounds stew meat
1 tablespoon vegetable oil
1 green pepper
12 pearl onions
12 baby carrots
12 small red potatoes
30 cherry tomatoes
4 tablespoons tapioca
2 tablespoons sugar
½ teaspoon salt
¼ teaspoon pepper

This dish is great to include in a party menu.
It's very simple, and you can set it to cook and leave it alone until it's done.

1. Sauté the meat in oil in a pan over medium heat until browned, then drain and transfer meat to the slow cooker.

2. Coarsely chop the green pepper. Peel the onions and scrub the carrots and potatoes.

3. Put the green pepper, onions, carrots, potatoes, tomatoes, tapioca, sugar, salt, and pepper in the slow cooker.

4. Cover and heat on a low setting for 4 to 5 hours.

Caraway Soup

Serves 6

Cooking time: 4–5 hours
Preparation time: 30 minutes
Attention: Minimal
Pot size: 3–5 quarts

3 pounds cabbage
1 cube chicken bouillon
3 cups chicken broth
½ cup diagonally sliced celery
1 tablespoon salt
½ tablespoon caraway seeds
¼ tablespoon pepper
1 tablespoon tapioca
1 cup cream

Caraway has a distinctive flavor that is delicious in soup.
Serve this with warm caraway bread on the side.

1. Coarsely chop the cabbage.

2. Dissolve the bouillon cube in the broth. Combine the vegetables, broth, salt, spices, and tapioca in the slow cooker.

3. Cover and heat on a low setting for 4 to 5 hours.

4. Half an hour before serving, stir in the cream.

Summer Meatball Soup

*For a nice change in texture, try adding a cup of cooked hominy
or butter beans or a half-cup of uncooked barley.*

Serves 8

Cooking time: 4–5 hours
Preparation time: 30 minutes
Attention: Minimal
Pot size: 3–5 quarts

*1 onion
3 carrots
2 stalks celery
1 zucchini
2 potatoes
½ teaspoon peppercorns
1 cup coarsely chopped
 tomatoes
6 cups beef stock
1½ pounds ground meat
½ teaspoon oregano
1 tablespoon oil*

1. Coarsely chop the onion and carrots. Slice the celery diagonally. Dice the zucchini and potatoes. Crack the peppercorns, but don't grind them.

2. Combine the vegetables, including the tomatoes, peppercorns, and stock in the slow cooker.

3. Mix the ground beef and oregano. Roll mixture into ½-inch meatballs. Sauté the meatballs in oil in a pan over high heat until browned. Drain the meatballs and transfer to the slow cooker.

4. Cover and heat on a low setting for 4 to 5 hours.

Delightful Dumplings

*You can add dumplings to nearly any soup or stew.
Simply add the dumplings right before you serve your guests.*

Yields about 6

Cooking time: 30 minutes
Preparation time: 15 minutes
Attention: Minimal
Pot size: 3–5 quarts

*1 egg
2 tablespoons sour milk
¼ teaspoon salt
¾ cup flour
1¼ teaspoons baking powder*

1. Lightly beat the egg, then stir in the milk and salt.

2. Sift the flour with the baking powder, then stir into the milk mixture.

3. Add the batter by large spoonfuls to the stew or soup once it is simmering.

4. Close the lid and leave it for 30 minutes before opening.

Cooking time: 4–5 hours
Preparation time: 30 minutes
Attention: Minimal
Pot size: 3–5 quarts

2 pounds stew meat
1 tablespoon oil
4 carrots
6 potatoes
1 onion
4 stalks celery
1 teaspoon salt
¼ teaspoon pepper
1 tablespoon parsley
½ teaspoon basil
¼ teaspoon marjoram
¼ teaspoon tarragon
2 tablespoons tapioca
1 teaspoon sugar
2 cups beef broth
1 small can V8 juice

Meat and Potato Stew

*Use your meat of choice to personalize this stew,
and serve with crusty bread for dipping.*

1. Cube the meat. Sauté the meat in oil in a pan over high heat until browned. Drain the meat and transfer it to the slow cooker.

2. Scrub and halve the carrots and potatoes. Quarter the onion and slice the celery.

3. Combine the vegetables, salt, spices, tapioca, sugar, broth, and juice in the slow cooker.

4. Cover and heat on a low setting for 4 to 5 hours. Do not lift cover while cooking.

Garnishes Galore

Go beyond croutons or cheese on your soup or stew. What about bow tie pasta? Squash blossoms? A dab of baked garlic paste? Be creative with garnishes and get reactions from your guests.

Pork Stew with Dumplings

You can use a biscuit mix to make dumplings (as shown in this recipe), or make Delightful Dumplings (page 85) from scratch.

Serves 6

Cooking time: 7–9 hours
Preparation time: 45 minutes
Attention: Moderate
Pot size: 3–5 quarts

6 small red potatoes
6 carrots
2 stalks celery
2 pounds pork stew meat
¼ cup flour
1½ teaspoons salt
½ teaspoon pepper
3 tablespoons vegetable oil
1 clove garlic
4 onions
4 cups water
2 teaspoons sugar
*1 teaspoon Worcestershire
    sauce*
1 bay leaf
1 small bunch fresh parsley
1 egg
1 cup buttermilk baking mix
3 tablespoons milk

1. Halve the potatoes and diagonally slice the carrots and celery. Arrange the vegetables in the slow cooker.

2. Cube the pork. Combine the flour, salt, and pepper and use to coat the meat cubes. Sauté the cubes in oil in a pan over medium heat until the meat is lightly browned. Mince the garlic and quarter the onions. Mix the garlic and onions with the meat cubes and arrange over the vegetables.

3. Mix the water, sugar, and Worcestershire sauce in a bowl. Pour into the slow cooker; add the bay leaf.

4. Cover and heat on a low setting for 6 to 8 hours.

5. To make the dumplings: Chop the parsley and beat the egg. Half an hour before serving, mix the parsley, egg, baking mix, and milk in a separate bowl, stirring only briefly. Drop by spoonfuls into the slow cooker. Cook with cover removed for 10 minutes. Replace cover and continue cooking for another 15 minutes.

No More Dull Dumplings

If you're making dumplings to top off your stew, soup, or other dish, don't use the plain old recipe. Try adding a dash of caraway seeds, thyme, poppy seeds, shredded cheese, or fresh parsley. A flavorful dumpling can make the dullest dish an adventure.

Beefy Pepper Stew

Try this stew with chicken or pork instead of beef.
If you have a hunter in the family, substitute moose or elk!

Serves 6

Cooking time: 4–5 hours
Preparation time: 30 minutes
Attention: Minimal
Pot size: 3–5 quarts

2 pounds stew beef
1 onion
3 cloves garlic
2 green bell peppers
1 teaspoon chili powder
2 tablespoons vegetable oil
1 pound tomatoes
2 dried corn tortillas or 15
    tortilla chips
2 cups water
½ teaspoon salt
2 bay leaves
1 teaspoon ground cloves
1 teaspoon ground oregano
¼ teaspoon pepper

1. Cube the beef. Coarsely chop the onion, garlic, and green peppers.

2. Sauté the beef, onion, garlic, green peppers, and chili powder in oil in a pan over medium heat until the beef is browned. Transfer to the slow cooker.

3. Coarsely chop the tomatoes. Crumble the corn tortillas. Add the tomatoes, tortillas, water, salt, and spices to the slow cooker.

4. Cover and heat on a low setting for 4 to 5 hours.

5. Before serving, remove the bay leaves.

Leftover Coffee

Add a dash of leftover coffee to gravy or stew for a beautiful color. Enough coffee can add an intriguing hint of flavor, as well. Your guests will detect something familiar, but they'll be unable to name it. Use different flavored coffees for unique effects.

Forest Mushroom Soup

Using both fresh and dried mushrooms adds more texture as well as more flavor to this dish. Try using fresh wild mushrooms, if available.

Serves 8

Cooking time: 4–5 hours
Preparation time: 30 minutes
Attention: Moderate
Pot size: 3–5 quarts

2 yellow onions
½ cup butter
2 pounds fresh mushrooms
½ cup dried mushrooms
¾ cup Madeira wine
4 cups chicken stock
½ teaspoon salt
¼ teaspoon pepper
2 cups heavy cream

1. Finely mince the onions. Sauté the onions in butter in a pan over low heat until the onions are soft.

2. Separate the stems from the caps of the fresh mushrooms. Mince the stems; thinly slice the caps. Add to the onions; sauté until soft. Transfer the onions and mushrooms to the slow cooker.

3. Cut the dried mushrooms into ½-inch strips. Rinse the dried mushroom strips under cold water and soak in the wine for an hour. Transfer the dried mushrooms to the slow cooker with a slotted spoon, setting aside the wine.

4. Add the chicken stock, salt, and pepper to the slow cooker. Cover and heat on low setting for 3 to 4 hours.

5. An hour before serving, lift out some of the mushrooms and onions and puree with the cream in a blender or food processor. Add the creamed mixture and the wine to the slow cooker.

Flour for Thickening
To thicken a thin sauce or soup, add ½ tablespoon flour with each cup of liquid. If you add 3 or 4 tablespoons flour per cup of liquid, the end result will be very thick. Whatever amount you use, mix the flour first with cold water or melted butter to make a paste, and then gradually stir into the hot liquid and let it swell while cooking.

Oriental Pumpkin Soup

Pumpkins are for more than making jack-o-lanterns!
They become sweet and tender when cooked, similar to autumn squash.

Cooking time: 4–5 hours
Preparation time: 30 minutes
Attention: Moderate
Pot size: 3–5 quarts

2 pounds fresh pumpkin
1 onion
2 cloves
2 tablespoons minced fresh
*   ginger*
3 cups chicken stock
½ teaspoon salt
¼ teaspoon cinnamon
½ teaspoon pepper
1 cup heavy cream

1. Peel and cube the pumpkin, removing the seeds and stringy core material. Peel the onion and press the cloves into the whole, peeled onion.

2. Arrange the pumpkin and onion in the slow cooker; sprinkle with the ginger. Add the stock, salt, and spices.

3. Cover and heat on a low setting for 3 to 4 hours.

4. Half an hour before serving, remove the onion with cloves and discard. Remove some pumpkin pieces with a slotted spoon and puree or mash the pumpkin with the cream. Return the creamed mixture to the slow cooker.

The Icing on the Soup

For a final, fancy touch, use your kitchen cookie cutters to punch out attractive shapes from vegetables that are suitable raw for a soup garnish, like sweet potato, turnip, or carrot. Cut thin slices to place in each bowl. They will float in the soup and add a nice bit of crunch for your guests.

chapter 6
hot sandwiches

Sausage and Sauerkraut Sandwich

Personalize this sandwich with venison, moose, or andouille sausage.
Also, choose German or Hungarian sauerkraut, or make your own.

Serves 6

Cooking time: 1–2 hours
Preparation time: 30 minutes
Attention: Minimal
Pot size: 3–5 quarts

1½ pounds bulk pork sausage
1 cup spiced sauerkraut
¼ pound Gruyère cheese
6 poppy seed rolls

1. Form the sausage meat into six patties and sauté in a pan over medium heat until browned and thoroughly cooked; drain. Drain the sauerkraut and thinly slice the cheese; split and toast the rolls.

2. Arrange the sandwich layers in this order: bottom of roll, sausage, sauerkraut, cheese, top of roll.

3. Wrap the sandwiches in foil and arrange on a trivet in the slow cooker. Pour water around the base of the trivet.

4. Cover and heat on a high setting for 1 to 2 hours.

Stromboli

*For a slight variation, substitute a nice olive relish
for the chopped olives on this sandwich.*

1. Thinly slice the beef. Sauté in butter in a pan over medium heat until lightly browned.

2. Toast the bread. Mince the olives. Thinly slice the ham and cheese.

3. Arrange the sandwich layers in this order: bread, beef, ham, olives, cheese, bread.

4. Wrap the sandwiches in foil and arrange on a trivet in the slow cooker. Pour water around the base of the trivet.

5. Cover and heat on a high setting for 1 to 2 hours.

Serves 6

Cooking time: 1–2 hours
Preparation time: 30 minutes
Attention: Minimal
Pot size: 3–5 quarts

½ pound roast beef
2 tablespoons butter
12 slices French bread
½ cup olives
½ pound ham
½ pound mozzarella cheese

Cheesy Melts

You can make the sandwich filling and prepare the rolls the day before your party, then assemble these sandwiches right before heating.

Yields 12

Cooking time: 1–2 hours
Preparation time: 30 minutes
Attention: Minimal
Pot size: 3–5 quarts

1½ pounds extra sharp
    Cheddar cheese
½ cup pitted black olives
¼ cup green chilies
1 onion
¾ cup tomato sauce
3 tablespoons olive oil
½ teaspoon black pepper
¼ teaspoon salt
12 large French rolls

1. Grate the cheese; slice the olives and chilies. Mince the onion.

2. Mix the cheese, olives, chilies, and onion with the tomato sauce, oil, pepper, and salt.

3. Cut the tops off the rolls. Stuff the rolls with the cheese mixture, replace the tops, and wrap the sandwiches in foil.

4. Arrange the wrapped sandwiches on a trivet or rack in the slow cooker. Pour water around the base of the trivet.

5. Cover and heat on a high setting for 1 to 2 hours.

Bagel and Muenster Cheese Sandwich

Don't worry about getting fresh bagels. The drier your bagels are, the more juice they'll absorb from the tomatoes and cheese.

Serves 6

Cooking time: 1–2 hours
Preparation time: 30 minutes
Attention: Minimal
Pot size: 3–5 quarts

6 bagels
2 tomatoes
½ pound Muenster cheese
½ pound cream cheese
1 onion

1. Slice the bagels, tomatoes, Muenster cheese, and cream cheese. Thinly slice the onion. Arrange the slices in this order: bagel, tomato, Muenster, onion, cream cheese, bagel.

2. Wrap the sandwiches in foil and arrange on a trivet in the slow cooker. Pour water around the base of the trivet.

3. Cover and heat on a high setting for 1 to 2 hours.

Steamers

If you don't have fresh buns available on party day, don't worry.
Stale buns will soften with the steam.

Yields 8

Cooking time: 1–2 hours
Preparation time: 30 minutes
Attention: Minimal
Pot size: 3–5 quarts

1 clove garlic
1 onion
1 pound ground beef
1 pound pork sausage
2 eggs
½ teaspoon salt
1 cup bread crumbs
¼ cup milk
8 hamburger buns
½ cup sliced pickles

1. Crush and mince the garlic; mince the onion. Mix the garlic and onion with the meat, eggs, salt, crumbs, and milk.

2. Form the mixture into 8 patties.

3. Briefly sear the patties on each side in a pan over high heat. Assemble the patties on hamburger buns, with pickles on each.

4. Wrap the sandwiches in aluminum foil. Arrange the wrapped sandwiches on a trivet or rack in the slow cooker. Pour water around the base of the trivet.

5. Cover and heat on a high setting for 1 to 2 hours.

For Future Use

Consider every leftover for use in future cooking. Cornbread, for example, can be used in many dishes. Pop it in the freezer to use later, as crumbs for meatloaf or in meat balls, giving regular old meatballs a whole new taste and texture.

Hot Corned Beef Sandwich

Serve with big dill pickles and cold cream soda on a hot afternoon when there's nothing better to do than spend time with good friends.

Serves 6

Cooking time: 1–2 hours
Preparation time: 30 minutes
Attention: Minimal
Pot size: 3–5 quarts

2 tablespoons horseradish
½ pound cream cheese
1 pound corned beef
12 slices rye bread

1. Cream the horseradish and the cream cheese together. Thinly slice the corned beef. Arrange the sandwich layers in this order: bread, beef, cheese, bread.

2. Wrap the sandwiches in foil and arrange on a trivet in the slow cooker. Pour water around the base of the trivet.

3. Cover and heat on a high setting for 1 to 2 hours.

Classic Reuben

These juicy sandwiches can be made ahead and frozen, then thawed before heating. You can make half-size sandwiches, as well.

Serves 6

Cooking time: 1–2 hours
Preparation time: 15 minutes
Attention: Minimal
Pot size: 3–5 quarts

12 slices rye bread
3 tablespoons butter
1 pound corned beef
½ pound Swiss cheese
1 pound sauerkraut
1 cup Russian dressing

1. Brown one side of each slice of bread in butter in a pan over medium heat.

2. Thinly slice the beef and the cheese. Drain sauerkraut until very dry. Arrange the sandwich layers in this order: bread (browned side out), beef, sauerkraut, dressing, cheese, bread.

3. Wrap the sandwiches in foil and arrange on a trivet in the slow cooker. Pour water around the base of the trivet.

4. Cover and heat on a high setting for 1 to 2 hours.

Crab and Mushroom Kaiser Roll

If you happen to have some fresh lobster, use it instead of crab.
Serve with a fresh green salad with vinaigrette.

1. Shred and blot dry the crabmeat, mince the mushrooms and parsley, and grate the cheese. Mix the crabmeat, mushrooms, parsley, cheese, mayonnaise, lemon juice, and herbs.

2. Split the rolls and toast the insides.

3. Arrange the sandwich layers in this order: bottom of roll (toasted side in), butter, crab mixture, almonds, butter, top of roll.

4. Wrap the sandwiches in foil and arrange on a trivet in the slow cooker. Pour water around the base of the trivet.

5. Cover and heat on a high setting for 1 to 2 hours.

Head for the Pantry

If you're short on time and your recipe calls for dried beans, go for the canned beans instead. For each cup of dried beans in a recipe, you can use 2½ cups canned. Likewise, 1 cup dry rice can be replaced by 3½ cups cooked rice (from your leftover takeout food, perhaps?), or 2 cups cooked rice if the recipe called for instant rice.

Serves 6

Cooking time: 1–2 hours
Preparation time: 30 minutes
Attention: Minimal
Pot size: 3–5 quarts

1 cup crabmeat
½ pound mushrooms
1 small bunch parsley
¼ pound Parmesan cheese
¾ cup mayonnaise
1 teaspoon lemon juice
⅛teaspoon rosemary
⅛ teaspoon thyme
⅛ teaspoon sage
6 Kaiser rolls
2 tablespoons butter
¼ cup toasted slivered almonds

Chicken and Gherkin Sandwich

Some people prefer sweet pickles, but dill pickles are the standard for guests. Use the baby gherkins; they have a nicer texture.

Serves 6

Cooking time: 1–2 hours
Preparation time: 30 minutes
Attention: Minimal
Pot size: 3–5 quarts

12 slices rye bread
½ pound cooked chicken
6 baby dill pickles
¼ pound mozzarella cheese
2 tablespoons butter
½ teaspoon salt
½ teaspoon pepper

1. Toast the bread on one side. Thinly slice the chicken, pickles, and cheese.

2. Arrange the sandwich layers in this order: bread (toasted side out), butter, chicken, salt, pepper, pickle, cheese, butter, bread.

3. Wrap the sandwiches in foil and arrange on a trivet in the slow cooker. Pour water around the base of the trivet.

4. Cover and heat on a high setting for 1 to 2 hours.

Ham and Swiss Croissant

Enhance this sandwich by using honey-baked ham, a fancy mustard, or cherry tomatoes. You can also add a few leaves of raw spinach.

Serves 6

Cooking time: 1–2 hours
Preparation time: 30 minutes
Attention: Minimal
Pot size: 3–5 quarts

6 croissants
2 tomatoes
½ pound Swiss cheese
½ pound ham
3 tablespoons mustard

1. Slice the croissants and the tomatoes. Thinly slice the cheese and ham.

2. Arrange the sandwich layers in this order: bottom of croissant, ham, cheese, mustard, ham, tomato, top of croissant.

3. Wrap the sandwiches in foil and arrange on a trivet in the slow cooker. Pour water around the base of the trivet.

4. Cover and heat on a high setting for 1 to 2 hours.

Bacon and Turkey Sandwich

Fresh slices of avocado are an excellent addition to this sandwich.

Serves 6

Cooking time: 1–2 hours
Preparation time: 30 minutes
Attention: Minimal
Pot size: 3–5 quarts

12 slices bacon
12 slices rye bread
2 tomatoes
½ pound turkey
¼ pound Gruyère cheese
¼ cup mayonnaise

1. Brown the bacon in a pan over medium heat until crispy; drain.

2. Toast the bread; slice the tomatoes. Thinly slice the turkey and cheese.

3. Arrange the sandwich layers in this order: bread, mayonnaise, turkey, bacon, tomato, cheese, bread.

4. Wrap the sandwiches in foil and arrange on a trivet in the slow cooker. Pour water around the base of the trivet.

5. Cover and heat on a high setting for 1 to 2 hours.

Tomato Heaven

Use dried tomato, which you can get in most grocery stores, to add intense dabs of sweet texture and bright color to any dish that calls for tomatoes. Open a bag and cut the entire batch into narrow strips or squares. After cutting and handling, store in the freezer, and they can be taken out and used as needed.

Steamed Turkey Sandwich

Choose a nice, dense sourdough, then leave it out for a day to dry before toasting. Also, try substituting goose or duck for turkey.

Serves 6

Cooking time: 1–2 hours
Preparation time: 30 minutes
Attention: Minimal
Pot size: 3–5 quarts

12 slices bacon
12 slices sourdough bread
3 tomatoes
½ pound turkey
½ pound Cheddar cheese
2 tablespoons butter
2 teaspoons mustard

1. Sauté the bacon in a pan over medium heat until crispy; drain.

2. Toast the bread; slice the tomatoes. Thinly slice the turkey and the cheese.

3. Arrange the sandwich layers in this order: bread, butter, turkey, cheese, bacon, tomato, mustard, butter, bread.

4. Wrap the sandwiches in foil and arrange on a trivet in the slow cooker. Pour water around the base of the trivet.

5. Cover and heat on a high setting for 1 to 2 hours.

Baked Ham, Gruyere, and Roquefort Sandwich

You can make these sandwiches on whole baguettes, then slice after assembly. You can also use this trick to make lots of tiny sandwiches.

Serves 6

Cooking time: 1–2 hours
Preparation time: 30 minutes
Attention: Minimal
Pot size: 3–5 quarts

2 long French baguettes
½ pound Gruyère cheese
½ pound ham
½ pound Roquefort cheese
2 tablespoons mayonnaise
3 tablespoons dry white wine
3 tablespoons butter

1. Cut the baguettes to yield 6 pieces, each 6 to 8 inches in length. Slice each lengthwise to open, then toast the insides.

2. Thinly slice the Gruyère and ham. Mince the Roquefort and blend with the mayonnaise and white wine.

3. Arrange the sandwich layers in this order: bottom of baguette, butter, Gruyère, ham, Roquefort spread, top of baguette.

4. Wrap the sandwiches in foil and arrange on a trivet in the slow cooker. Pour water around the base of the trivet.

5. Cover and heat on a high setting for 1 to 2 hours.

Instant Sauce

Do you have leftover sauce after your party? Freeze sauces in ice cube trays, then pop out the cubes later and seal in plastic bags or freezer containers. Take out one or four or twelve cubes later, as needed, for individual servings or sandwiches.

Saucisson en Croute

Use a nice chewy roll for this hot sandwich.
Also, try lengths of French bread, or roll the sausages in pita bread.

Serves 6

Cooking time: 1–2 hours
Preparation time: 30 minutes
Attention: Minimal
Pot size: 3–5 quarts

6 spicy Italian sausages
6 long sourdough rolls
2 tablespoons Dijon mustard

1. Sauté the sausages in a pan over medium heat until browned and thoroughly cooked; drain.

2. Cut off the tips of the rolls. Use the handle of a wooden spoon to hollow out the center of the roll. Dip the sausages in the mustard and insert each into a roll.

3. Wrap the sandwiches in foil and arrange on a trivet in the slow cooker. Pour water around the base of the trivet.

4. Cover and heat on a high setting for 1 to 2 hours.

Sauerkraut and Bratwurst Roll

*These can be messy, but it's worth it. You can substitute
caraway rye bread for pita—just split the bratwurst lengthwise.*

Serves 6

Cooking time: 1–2 hours
Preparation time: 30 minutes
Attention: Minimal
Pot size: 3–5 quarts

1 apple
1½ pounds sauerkraut
1 tablespoon caraway seeds
2 tablespoons oil
6 bratwurst
1 tablespoon butter
½ cup white wine
2 tablespoons Dijon mustard
6 whole-wheat pita loaves

1. Core and chop the apple; drain the sauerkraut. Sauté the sauerkraut, apple, and caraway seeds in the oil in a pan over medium heat until the apple is soft and the liquids are reduced.

2. Sauté the bratwurst in butter in a pan over medium heat until browned on both sides; drain. Add the wine and continue to sauté over medium heat until the liquid has evaporated.

3. Roll each bratwurst, with sauerkraut and mustard, into a pita loaf.

4. Wrap the sandwiches in foil and arrange on a trivet in the slow cooker. Pour water around the base of the trivet.

5. Cover and heat on a high setting for 1 to 2 hours.

Why Cook Slowly?

Foods with a lot of sugar, or dried fruit, which is dense with fruit sugars, should be cooked at lower temperatures so the sugar won't scorch. Large pieces of meat should also be cooked at lower temperatures, so the heat has time to reach the center of the meat without burning the outside.

Classic Sloppy Joes

Serves 8

Cooking time: 3–4 hours
Preparation time: 30 minutes
Attention: Minimal
Pot size: 3–5 quarts

2 onions
1 clove garlic
2 tablespoons oil
1 pound ground beef
1 pound ground pork
¼ cup molasses
½ cup cider vinegar
½ cup tomato paste
¼ teaspoon salt
½ teaspoon black pepper

*Make this sandwich filling at your convenience, then chill or freeze.
Reheat in your slow cooker just before your party.*

1. Thinly slice the onions; crush and mince the garlic. Sauté the onions and garlic in oil in a pan over low heat until soft. Transfer to the slow cooker.

2. Brown the meat in the same pan over medium heat; drain. Add the meat, molasses, vinegar, tomato paste, salt, and pepper to the slow cooker.

3. Cover and heat on a low setting for 3 to 4 hours.

Quick Tomato Peeling

Not everyone likes peeled tomatoes. Sometimes the presence of the peels adds just a bit more color and texture. But if you do peel, there is a helpful trick. Arrange the tomatoes in a bowl. Cover them with boiling water for two minutes, then drain. This will loosen the skins for easier peeling.

Mexican Sloppy Joes

Try replacing the pinto beans with black beans or garbanzos for a different texture and flavor. Serve with tortilla chips and salsa.

Serves 8

Cooking time: 3–4 hours
Preparation time: 30 minutes
Attention: Minimal
Pot size: 3–5 quarts

1. Thinly slice the onion; crush and mince the garlic. Sauté the onion and garlic in oil in a pan over low heat until the onion is soft. Transfer to the slow cooker.

2. Sauté the meat in a pan over medium heat until browned; drain. Add to the slow cooker.

3. Slice the olives. Add to the slow cooker, along with the jalapeno peppers, chilies, chili pepper, salt, beans, vinegar, and tomato sauce.

4. Cover and heat on a low setting for 3 to 4 hours.

5. Before serving, grate the cheese and stir in.

1 onion
1 clove garlic
2 tablespoons oil
1 pound ground beef
1 pound ground pork
½ cup pitted black olives
¼ cup sliced jalapeno
  peppers
¼ cup sliced green chilies
¼ teaspoon chili pepper
¼ teaspoon salt
1 cup cooked pinto beans
½ cup red wine vinegar
½ cup tomato sauce
¼ pound Monterey Jack
  cheese

When to Salt?

If you're in a hurry when you're cooking dried beans, add salt after cooking, not before. If salt is added before cooking, it will slow things down.

Oriental Sloppy Joes

Serve this filling on sesame seed buns or in pita pockets. Provide thinly sliced pickled ginger root and some fresh green onion shoots for toppings.

Serves 8

Cooking time: 2–3 hours
Preparation time: 30 minutes
Attention: Minimal
Pot size: 3–5 quarts

1 onion
1 clove garlic
2 tablespoons sesame oil
1 pound ground beef
1 pound ground pork
¼ cup water chestnuts
3 green onions
1 teaspoon cornstarch
2 tablespoons water
½ cup rice vinegar
¼ cup soy sauce
¼ teaspoon salt

1. Thinly slice the onion; crush and mince the garlic. Sauté the onion and garlic in the sesame oil in a pan over low heat. Transfer, with oil, to the slow cooker.

2. Sauté the meat in a pan over medium heat until browned; drain. Add to the slow cooker.

3. Slice the water chestnuts and green onions. Dissolve the cornstarch in water; stir in the vinegar, soy sauce, and salt. Add the sliced vegetables and the starch mixture to the slow cooker.

4. Cover and heat on a low setting for 2 to 3 hours.

Serving Sizes
A good party strategy is to keep the bowls and plates small. This will give guests more reason to move around the party and mingle with different people, while having the chance to try all of your different foods a little at a time.

chapter 7
vegetables

Farmer Peas

For the best flavor, use fresh peas or spring peapods in this dish.
This goes well with chicken or seafood.

Cooking time: 2–3 hours
Preparation time: 30 minutes
Attention: Minimal
Pot size: 3–5 quarts

1 onion
6 small carrots
1 head romaine lettuce
2 cups fresh green peas
12 asparagus tips
1 cup beef broth
1 cup water
½ teaspoon salt
½ teaspoon sugar
3 tablespoons butter

1. Coarsely chop the onion, carrots, and lettuce.

2. Combine the chopped vegetables with the peas, asparagus tips, broth, water, salt, sugar, and butter in the slow cooker.

3. Cover and heat on a high setting for 2 to 3 hours.

Plan Ahead

Any time you cook vegetables, save the broth and freeze it. The next time you make rice, use the vegetable broth as a flavorful liquid base and get some extra vitamins out of the bargain.

Carrots in Dill and Wine

The aromatic flavor of dill blends well with carrot.
If you have fresh dill, save some to add just before serving.

Serves 6

Cooking time: 3–4 hours
Preparation time: 30 minutes
Attention: Moderate
Pot size: 3–5 quarts

1 onion
2 cloves garlic
8 medium carrots
½ cup chicken broth
½ teaspoon dried dill weed
¼ teaspoon salt
1 tablespoon lemon juice
2 tablespoons cornstarch
2 tablespoons cold water
½ cup dry white wine

1. Mince the onion; crush the garlic. Cut the carrots into small sticks.

2. Combine the onion, garlic, carrots, broth, dill weed, salt, and lemon juice in the slow cooker.

3. Cover and heat on a high setting for 2 to 3 hours.

4. An hour before serving, mix the cornstarch into the cold water, stir into the slow cooker, and turn the temperature to low. Add the wine.

Kernel Count
How many cups of corn kernels are on one ear? Good question.
A dozen ears of corn contain about two cups of cut corn kernels.

Home Sweet Potatoes

This is possibly the simplest potato recipe you'll ever use.
There's no need to even peel the potatoes!

Serves 6

Cooking time: 5–6 hours
Preparation time: 15 minutes
Attention: Minimal
Pot size: 3–5 quarts

6 sweet potatoes
3 tablespoons butter
¼ cup brown sugar

1. Wash the potatoes, and put them in the slow cooker while still wet.

2. Cover and heat on a low setting for 5 to 6 hours.

3. Before serving, top with butter and brown sugar.

Slow Vegetables

Some vegetables, like potatoes, take longer to cook than others. Try placing those vegetables at the bottom of the slow cooker, where they will cook the most intensely and be more likely to keep up with the others.

Stuffed Baked Potatoes

Did you know you can freeze baked potatoes?
Keep a tub of these in the freezer, then thaw and restuff as needed.

Serves 6

Cooking time: 1–2 hours
Preparation time: 15 minutes
Attention: Minimal
Pot size: 3–5 quarts

¼ pound Cheddar cheese
6 baked potatoes
1 cup sour cream
½ teaspoon salt
½ teaspoon pepper

1. Shred the cheese. Halve the potatoes. Scoop most of the insides of the potatoes into a mixing bowl. Add the sour cream, cheese, salt, and pepper and mix well. Return the mixture to the potatoes.

2. Wrap the potatoes in foil and arrange on a trivet in the slow cooker. Pour water around the base of the trivet.

3. Cover and heat on a high setting for 1 to 2 hours.

Cleaning Cheese Graters

Grating cheese isn't so bad. It's the cleanup that takes time, and hot water just melts the cheese and makes it harder to remove. Instead, after grating the cheese for your recipe, grate a raw potato. This will push the cheese out of the grater holes and make it easier to clean.

Cooking time: 2–3 hours
Preparation time: 30 minutes
Attention: Minimal
Pot size: 3–5 quarts

2 pounds baby carrots
½ pound yellow squash
¼ cup butter
3 tablespoons brown sugar
1 teaspoon ground cinnamon
½ teaspoon ground cumin
¼ teaspoon cayenne pepper
¼ teaspoon pepper
½ teaspoon salt
2 cups peas
1¼ cups orange juice

Spiced Orange Vegetables

*For extra zing, you can set aside a dash of the fresh orange juice
to add at the very end, just before serving.*

1. Cube the squash.

2. Melt the butter in a pan and stir in the sugar, spices, and salt; add the carrots, squash, and peas and stir until coated.

3. Transfer the vegetable mix to the slow cooker. Add the orange juice.

4. Cover and heat on a medium setting for 2 to 3 hours.

Cooking time: 3–4 hours
Preparation time: 30 minutes
Attention: Minimal
Pot size: 3–5 quarts

2 yellow onions
½ cup extra-virgin olive oil
4 pounds tomatoes
1 can tomato paste
2 tablespoons fresh basil
½ teaspoon oregano
1 teaspoon salt
1 tablespoon black pepper
2 cups water
5 cloves garlic
½ cup cilantro

Mrs. Bertolini's Tomato Sauce

*Ripe plum tomatoes work best in this sauce.
The result will be far better than if you use canned tomatoes.*

1. Finely chop the onions. Sauté in oil in a pan over low heat until the onions are tender.

2. Chop the tomatoes. Add the tomatoes, paste, basil, oregano, salt, pepper, and water to the slow cooker.

3. Cover and heat on a low setting for 3 to 4 hours.

4. Finely mince the garlic. Coarsely chop the cilantro. Half an hour before serving, add the garlic and cilantro to the slow cooker.

Dallas Beans

*This is the dish to serve when having friends over to watch old Westerns.
Serve with grilled hamburgers and root beer.*

1. Cover the beans with water and soak overnight in the slow cooker, then drain and discard the water.

2. Coarsely chop the onion, garlic, and salt pork. Add to the beans in the slow cooker and stir in ½ cup water.

3. Cover and heat on a low setting for 6 to 8 hours.

4. Chop the green pepper and tomatoes. Two hours before serving, add the green pepper, tomatoes, white pepper, salt, pepper sauce, and sugar to the slow cooker.

Serves 9

Cooking time: 8–10 hours
Preparation time: 30 minutes
Attention: Minimal
Pot size: 3–5 quarts

2 cups dry pinto beans
1 onion
1 clove garlic
¼ pound salt pork
½ cup water
1 green pepper
5 tomatoes
¼ teaspoon white pepper
1 teaspoon salt
6 drops hot pepper sauce
2 tablespoons sugar

Red Cabbage with Wine

*Red cabbage becomes sweet and tender after slow cooking,
and in this recipe, the red wine helps it retain its rich red color.*

1. Finely slice the red cabbage.

2. Combine the cabbage, salt, pepper, broth, and oil in the slow cooker.

3. Cover and heat on a low setting for 3 to 4 hours.

4. An hour before serving, add the wine.

Serves 6

Cooking time: 4–5 hours
Preparation time: 15 minutes
Attention: Minimal
Pot size: 3–5 quarts

1 head red cabbage
1 teaspoon salt
½ teaspoon coarsely ground black pepper
2 cups beef broth
1 tablespoon vegetable oil
1 cup red wine

Spiced Tomatoes

*This tangy and colorful side dish goes well with beef or pork,
and it can be served hot or cold.*

Serves 6

Cooking time: 2–3 hours
Preparation time: 30 minutes
Attention: Minimal
Pot size: 3–5 quarts

*2 pounds red and yellow pear
  tomatoes*
1 teaspoon ground cloves
1 teaspoon ground allspice
*1 teaspoon coarsely ground
  black pepper*
1 tablespoon sugar
2 cups cider vinegar

1. Pierce the tomatoes and arrange them in the slow cooker.

2. Sprinkle the tomatoes with the spices. Dissolve the sugar in the vinegar and pour it over the tomatoes.

3. Cover and heat on a low setting for 2 to 3 hours.

Sweet and Sour Beans

*This multibean dish keeps well in the refrigerator
and can be served hot or cold. It also goes well with sandwiches.*

Serves 8

Cooking time: 3–4 hours
Preparation time: 30 minutes
Attention: Minimal
Pot size: 3–5 quarts

4 slices bacon
1 onion
1 clove garlic
1 pound cooked lima beans
1 1-pound can baked beans
1 pound cooked kidney beans
¼ cup brown sugar
1 teaspoon prepared mustard
1 teaspoon salt
¼ cup vinegar

1. Sauté the bacon in a pan over medium heat until crisp. Drain the bacon. Transfer 2 tablespoons of the drippings to the slow cooker.

2. Coarsely chop the onion and mince the garlic. Drain all three kinds of beans. Add the onion, garlic, and beans to the slow cooker.

3. Crumble the bacon. Add the bacon, sugar, mustard, salt, and vinegar to the slow cooker.

4. Cover and heat on a low setting for 3 to 4 hours.

Spinach Callaloo

Wash the spinach well to remove any sand or grit.
A dash of vinegar in the rinse water will help get rid of insects, too.

Serves 6

Cooking time: 3–4 hours
Preparation time: 30 minutes
Attention: Minimal
Pot size: 3–5 quarts

¼ pound salt pork
2 onions
½ pound pork
4 cups chicken broth
½ teaspoon salt
1 tablespoon ground thyme
½ teaspoon black pepper
⅛ teaspoon bottled pepper
  sauce
1½ pounds fresh spinach

1. Mince the salt pork. Heat the salt pork in a pan over medium heat until browned; drain off all except 2 tablespoons of fat.

2. Slice the onions and cube the pork. Add the onions and pork to the browned salt pork; heat in the pan over medium heat until the pork cubes are browned. Drain.

3. Add the onions, pork, broth, salt, spices, and pepper sauce to the slow cooker.

4. Cover and heat on a low setting for 3 to 4 hours.

5. Trim the spinach, finely chopping large stems and cutting leaves into 2-inch strips. An hour before serving, add the spinach to the slow cooker.

Easy Onions

You can save time with high-efficiency onion prep. Peel and quarter onions, then lay them one layer deep on a pan in the freezer. As soon as they freeze, pack them in bags. Use as needed, frozen or thawed. You can cut them while still frozen if you have a sharp knife.

Simple Beans

Yields about 4 cups

Cooking time: 4–6 hours
Preparation time: 30 minutes
Attention: Minimal
Pot size: 3–5 quarts

1 cup dried beans
2 cups water

1. Soak the beans in water overnight, then drain and rinse.

2. Add soaked beans and 2 cups fresh water to the slow cooker.

3. Cover and heat on a low setting for 8 to 10 hours or overnight.

Easy Pickle Beans

This is a good Super Bowl menu item. It's easy to make, very popular,
and best of all, you can watch the game while it cooks.

Serves 8

Cooking time: 3–4 hours
Preparation time: 30 minutes
Attention: Minimal
Pot size: 3–5 quarts

6 slices bacon
½ onion
½ cup sweet pickle relish
4 cups baked beans
2 tablespoons molasses
½ teaspoon salt

1. Cut the bacon into 1-inch pieces. Sauté in a pan over medium heat until crisp. Transfer the bacon pieces to the slow cooker, leaving the drippings in the pan.

2. Coarsely chop the onion. Sauté the onion in the pan with the bacon drippings until the onion is tender but not brown. Drain; transfer the onion to the slow cooker.

3. Drain the relish. Add the relish, beans, molasses, and salt to the slow cooker.

4. Cover and heat on a low setting for 3 to 4 hours.

chapter 8
beef, pork, and lamb

Pop Chops

If you don't like lemon-lime soda pop, try your favorite in this recipe.
Soda is acidic, like vinegar, and helps tenderize the meat.

Serves 6

Cooking time: 6–8 hours
Preparation time: 30 minutes
Attention: Minimal
Pot size: 3–5 quarts

6 pork chops
3 tablespoons flour
2 tablespoons oil
1 can lemon-lime soda pop
¼ cup catsup
1 teaspoon brown sugar
1 teaspoon Worcestershire sauce
1 teaspoon vinegar
1 teaspoon salt
¼ teaspoon dry mustard powder
¼ teaspoon celery seed
⅛ teaspoon pepper
¼ cup coarsely chopped onion

1. Coat the pork chops in the flour. Sauté in oil in a pan over medium heat until browned, then drain.

2. Mix the soda pop, catsup, sugar, Worcestershire sauce, vinegar, salt, and spices in a small bowl.

3. Arrange the pork chops in the slow cooker, sprinkling each with chopped onion and the soda pop mixture.

4. Cover and heat on a low setting for 6 to 8 hours.

Corned Beef Dinner

Use slices of leftover corned beef from this recipe
to make a Classic Reuben (page 96).

Serves 8

Cooking time: 6–8 hours
Preparation time: 30 minutes
Attention: Minimal
Pot size: 3–5 quarts

6 carrots
6 potatoes
1 head cabbage
2 onions
2 cloves garlic
6 whole cloves
2 bay leaves
4 pounds corned beef brisket
1 cup water

1. Peel and halve the carrots and potatoes. Cut the cabbage into 8 wedges. Arrange the cut vegetables in the bottom of the slow cooker.

2. Slice the onions and mince the garlic. Mix with the cloves. Put half the onion mixture and one bay leaf on the vegetables in the slow cooker.

3. Cut the beef into serving-size slices. Arrange on the onion mixture, then cover with the remaining onion mixture and last bay leaf. Add the water.

4. Cover and heat on a low setting for 6 to 8 hours.

Don't Forget Turnips

Turnips, common in some cultures but forgotten by others, are a naturally sweet root and are delicious in curries and soups. Avoid adding salt before cooking with turnips, as they will lose their sweetness. Add salt only at the end, to flavor.

New England Boiled Dinner

Boiling the salt pork before cooking will eliminate excess salt,
but it won't decrease the flavor. Serve with black bread and icy curls of butter.

Serves 12

Cooking time: 6–8 hours
Preparation time: 30 minutes
Attention: Minimal
Pot size: 3–5 quarts

½ *pound salt pork*
5 *pounds beef brisket*
3 *turnips*
3 *beets*
3 *carrots*
½ *head cabbage*
½ *teaspoon salt*
2 *cups water*
1 *bouquet garni*

1. Cube the salt pork and boil in water in a pan over high heat for 10 minutes. Drain; discard the water. Transfer the salt pork to the slow cooker.

2. Cut the beef into long strips. Peel and quarter the turnips, beets, and carrots. Chop the cabbage. Arrange the meat and vegetables in the slow cooker.

3. Add the salt, water, and bouquet garni.

4. Cover and heat on a low setting for 6 to 8 hours.

5. Before serving, remove the bouquet garni.

Making Shapes

Tired of 1-inch cubes of vegetables and meats? Use small metal cookie cutters to punch out triangles, circles, or diamond shapes. Check your local art supply store for tiny cookie cutters used to cut out clay shapes. Get the metal ones. They may bend but they shouldn't break.

Garlic Lamb

Have a couple of jars of minced garlic on hand at all times. It lasts indefinitely in the refrigerator, and your hands won't smell like garlic all day.

Serves 6

Cooking time: 6–8 hours
Preparation time: 30 minutes
Attention: Minimal
Pot size: 3–5 quarts

5 cloves garlic
5 pounds lamb
4 tablespoons olive oil
2 onions
6 potatoes
½ teaspoon salt
½ teaspoon pepper
1 cup water
1 bouquet garni
½ cup parsley

1. Mince the garlic. Cut the lamb meat into long strips. Sauté the lamb and garlic in oil in a pan over medium heat until the lamb is browned.

2. Slice the onions. Peel and quarter the potatoes. Arrange the onions and potatoes, then the lamb, in the slow cooker, placing the potatoes at the bottom.

3. Add salt, pepper, water, and bouquet garni to the slow cooker.

4. Cover and heat on a low setting for 6 to 8 hours.

5. Chop the parsley. Before serving, stir the parsley into the slow cooker.

Tenderizing Meat

Use chemistry to your advantage here. Cover your meat with an acidic liquid such as tomato juice, pineapple juice, dry wine, or vinegar, and let it stand for an hour or more before cooking. The acid breaks down collagen, the toughest protein in the meat, making the meat softer.

Leo's Savory Ham

Soaking the ham before cooking will draw out some of the salt, giving the ham a milder, sweeter flavor.

Serves 6

Cooking time: 6–8 hours
Preparation time: 30 minutes
Attention: Minimal
Pot size: 3–5 quarts

4 pounds smoked ham
5 carrots
¼ pound celery tops
2 bay leaves
½ teaspoon thyme
½ teaspoon sage
½ teaspoon basil
¼ teaspoon mace
¼ teaspoon cloves
8 whole peppercorns
3 tablespoons molasses
1½ cups water
½ cup Madeira wine

1. Cube the ham. Soak the ham in cold water for 12 hours in the refrigerator. Drain and discard the water.

2. Slice the carrots in 1-inch sections; chop the celery tops.

3. Arrange the carrots, celery, ham, and spices in the slow cooker, in that order. Mix the molasses into the water and pour into the slow cooker.

4. Cover and heat on a low setting for 6 to 8 hours.

5. Half an hour before serving, add the Madeira wine. Remove the bay leaves before serving.

Simple Beef with Vegetables

Turnips become sweet and tender when cooked. For efficient cooking, try putting the harder root vegetables, like turnips, at the bottom of your slow cooker.

Serves 6

Cooking time: 6–8 hours
Preparation time: 30 minutes
Attention: Minimal
Pot size: 3–5 quarts

2 onions
2 leeks
½ head cabbage
2 stalks celery
4 pounds stew beef
4 carrots
2 turnips
½ teaspoon salt
12 peppercorns
1 cup water

1. Coarsely chop the onions. Slice the leeks and quarter the cabbage. Diagonally slice the celery. Cut the beef, carrots, and turnips into 1-inch sections.

2. Combine the cut vegetables and meat in the slow cooker. Add the salt, peppercorns, and water.

3. Cover and heat on a low setting for 6 to 8 hours.

Beef in Red

Wine, like vinegar, helps tenderize meats by breaking down the meat tissue. Use your red wine of choice for this recipe.

Serves 6

Cooking time: 6–8 hours
Preparation time: 30 minutes
Attention: Minimal
Pot size: 3–5 quarts

5 pounds beef
2 onions
2 carrots
1 cup red wine
1 cup water
1 bouquet garni
2 tablespoons butter
2 tablespoons flour
12 small red potatoes

1. Cube the beef. Slice the onions and carrots. Combine the beef, onions, carrots, wine, water, and bouquet garni. Cover and marinate for 24 hours in the refrigerator.

2. After marinating, transfer the beef to a pan; set aside the liquids and vegetables.

3. Sauté the beef in the butter in a pan over medium heat until the meat is browned. Stir in the flour and mix while heating until the flour browns.

4. Halve the potatoes. Combine the beef marinade with vegetables, and potatoes in the slow cooker, arranging the potatoes on the bottom.

5. Cover and heat on a low setting for 6 to 8 hours.

Great Garni

How do you make a bouquet garni? Just tie 2 sprigs of parsley, 1 bay leaf, and 1 sprig of thyme by the stems, or wrap them in cheesecloth. After cooking, you should fish the bundled herbs out of your slow cooker and discard them before serving.

Peppery Pork Pot

This goes well with chewy wheat dinner rolls. Serve them warm in a basket, wrapped in a soft cotton cloth to contain the heat.

Serves 6

Cooking time: 6–8 hours
Preparation time: 30 minutes
Attention: Minimal
Pot size: 3–5 quarts

4 onions
1 stalk celery
2 leeks
1 green bell pepper
¼ pound butter
2 tablespoons flour
2 pounds pork
1 pound potatoes
1 tablespoon black
    peppercorns
8 cups chicken stock
1 bouquet garni
½ teaspoon salt
¼ cup parsley

1. Chop the onions, slice the celery and leeks, and dice the green pepper. Sauté the onions, celery, leeks, and green pepper in butter in a pan over medium heat until soft. Stir in the flour until it is well mixed in.

2. Cube the pork and potatoes. Arrange the ingredients in the slow cooker: potatoes first, then pork, and then the onion mixture. Freshly grind some peppercorns and sprinkle them over the ingredients as they are added.

3. Add the stock, bouquet garni, and salt.

4. Cover and heat on a low setting for 6 to 8 hours.

5. Chop the parsley. Half an hour before serving, stir in the parsley.

Slow Cooker Placement
If you have enough outlets, put your slow cookers in "party position" before you start cooking. This way, you don't have to carry full, hot cookers and risk getting burned or spilling your delicious creations right before guests arrive.

Spicy Ham

This ham has enough spice for an entire dinner, so serve it with something mild. Try it with boiled red potatoes and crusty French bread.

1. Soak the ham overnight in cold water. Drain and discard the water. Cut the meat into 1-inch cubes.

2. Mix the spices (except bay leaf), sugar, jelly, and mustard in a small bowl.

3. Slice the onion and carrots. Arrange the carrots and onion at the bottom of the slow cooker, then sprinkle with half of the spice mixture.

4. Arrange the ham over the cut vegetables in the slow cooker and sprinkle with the remaining spice mixture. Add the water and bay leaf.

5. Cover and heat on a low setting for 6 to 8 hours. Before serving, remove the bay leaf.

Serves 10

Cooking time: 6–8 hours
Preparation time: 30 minutes
Attention: Minimal
Pot size: 3–5 quarts

5 pounds ham
3 cloves
1 teaspoon black peppercorns
½ teaspoon allspice
¼ teaspoon ground coriander
2 tablespoons brown sugar
2 tablespoons cranberry or quince jelly
1 teaspoon whole-grain mustard
1 small onion
2 carrots
2 cups water
1 bay leaf

Pull-Apart Pork

This is excellent on sandwiches, or by itself. It also freezes well and can be stored in single-serving containers for quick meals.

Cooking time: 6–8 hours
Preparation time: 30 minutes
Attention: Minimal
Pot size: 3–5 quarts

2 pounds pork stew meat
2 yellow onions
1 tablespoon oil
4 cloves garlic
4 pounds tomatoes
4 teaspoons hot chili powder
¼ teaspoon ground
   cinnamon
¼ teaspoon cayenne pepper
1 tablespoon dried oregano
1 tablespoon ground cumin
½ teaspoon salt
¼ cup cider vinegar
½ cup golden raisins

1. Cube the pork and coarsely chop the onions. Sauté the meat and onions in the oil in a pan over medium heat until the meat is lightly browned.

2. Mince the garlic and chop the tomatoes; mix the tomatoes and garlic.

3. Mix the spices, salt, vinegar, and raisins in a small bowl.

4. Put half of the tomato mixture in the bottom of the slow cooker. Sprinkle with one-quarter of the spice mixture. Put the meat mixture over this, and sprinkle with half of the spice mixture. Put the remaining tomato mixture on top of the meat, and sprinkle with the remaining spice mixture.

5. Cover and heat on a low setting for 6 to 8 hours.

Be Creative with Carrots

For a quick vegetable dish with some zing, sprinkle some sugar and a dab of horseradish on your cooked carrots. These flavors each hit different sets of your taste buds, and together they can improve most cooked vegetables.

Fennel Chops

These chops are very flavorful; all you need is a simple side of white rice or fresh homemade bread.

1. Crush the garlic and salt into a paste; rub the paste over the chops.

2. Sauté the chops in olive oil in a pan over medium heat until lightly browned. Put the chops, pan drippings, fennel seed, and white wine in the slow cooker.

3. Cover and heat on a low setting for 3 to 4 hours.

Better Butter

Set out some delicious herbed or spiced butter next to the bread, potatoes, or vegetables on your table. Blend 2 tablespoons of fresh tarragon, dill weed, or dried rosemary or 2 teaspoons of fresh minced garlic or crushed peppercorns into ¼ pound of butter.

Serves 6

Cooking time: 3–4 hours
Preparation time: 30 minutes
Attention: Minimal
Pot size: 3–5 quarts

2 cloves garlic
½ teaspoon salt
6 pork chops
2 tablespoons olive oil
1 tablespoon fennel seed
1 cup white wine

Pepper Chops

*This is a really simple recipe for a great dish.
Try this with a chilled side like coleslaw or fruit salad.*

1. Slice the onion and rub the chops with the salt and peppercorns. Sauté the chops and onion in oil in a pan over medium heat until lightly browned. Put chops, onions, and water in the slow cooker.

2. Cover and heat on a low setting for 3 to 4 hours.

Serves 6

Cooking time: 3–4 hours
Preparation time: 30 minutes
Attention: Minimal
Pot size: 3–5 quarts

1 onion
6 pork chops
3 teaspoons seasoning salt
2 teaspoons cracked black
*   peppercorns*
2 tablespoons olive oil
½ cup water

Slow Beef Roast

Serves 8

Cooking time: 6–8 hours
Preparation time: 30 minutes
Attention: Minimal
Pot size: 3–5 quarts

1 8-ounce can tomato sauce
2 tablespoons Worcestershire
    sauce
½ cup catsup
2 tablespoons brown sugar
2 tablespoons cider vinegar
½ teaspoon coarsely ground
    pepper
1 onion
1 clove garlic
3 slices raw bacon
4 pounds beef rump roast

*This dish cooks all day, letting you relax for a while before you entertain
in the evening. For a variation, try substituting goose for the roast.*

1. Mix the sauces, catsup, sugar, vinegar, and pepper in a small bowl.

2. Chop the onion and mince the garlic. Mix the onion and garlic. Cut the bacon into 1-inch pieces, and cut the roast into serving-size pieces.

3. Put half of the onion mixture in the bottom of the slow cooker, and sprinkle it with one-fourth of the sauce mixture.

4. Arrange the beef and bacon on top of this, and cover it with half of the remaining sauce mixture. Put the remaining onion mixture on the top, and cover with the rest of the sauce mixture.

5. Cover and heat on a low setting for 6 to 8 hours.

Simple Beef and Potatoes

Serves 6

Cooking time: 6–8 hours
Preparation time: 15 minutes
Attention: Minimal
Pot size: 3–5 quarts

2 pounds baby carrots
1 onion
6 potatoes
3 stalks celery
3 pounds beef roast
3 cubes beef bouillon
½ cup water

*Consider this a basic recipe, and add your own personality to it.
Use wild game instead of beef, or add your favorite herbs.*

1. Thinly slice the carrots, onion, potatoes, and celery. Transfer to the slow cooker in that order. Cube the beef, and arrange on top of the vegetables.

2. Dissolve the bouillon cubes in the water and pour over the beef.

3. Cover and heat on a low setting for 6 to 8 hours.

Peppery Southwestern Beef

Hot, sweet, spicy, smoky, and tart; this beef has it all. With slow cooking, flavors blend and mature over time to create something unique.

1. Mix the catsup, sauces, liquid smoke, spices, celery salt, sugar, juice, and mustard in a small bowl.

2. Chop the onion and mince the garlic; mix the onion and garlic. Put half of the onion mixture in the bottom of the slow cooker. Add the water. Sprinkle the onions with one-fourth of the sauce mixture.

3. Cut the meat into serving-size pieces. Arrange it in the slow cooker, on top of the onion and sauce layers. Sprinkle the meat with half of the remaining sauce mixture.

4. Put the remaining onion mixture and sauce mixture on top of the meat.

5. Cover and heat on a low setting for 6 to 8 hours.

Serves 8

Cooking time: 6–8 hours
Preparation time: 30 minutes
Attention: Minimal
Pot size: 3–5 quarts

½ cup catsup
1 tablespoon soy sauce
2 teaspoons Worcestershire
    sauce
1 tablespoon liquid smoke
¼ teaspoon red pepper flakes
¼ teaspoon ground nutmeg
2 teaspoons coarsely ground
    pepper
2 teaspoons celery salt
¼ cup brown sugar
1 tablespoon fresh lemon juice
1 tablespoon prepared mustard
1 onion
1 clove garlic
½ cup water
4 pounds rump roast

Beef Brisket with Beer

If you have time, you can brown the coated beef slices and onion in a tablespoon of olive oil before cooking.

1. Cut the beef into serving-size pieces and rub with seasoning salt and brown sugar. Thinly slice the onion. Arrange the beef and onion in the slow cooker and add the beer.

2. Cover and heat on a low setting for 6 to 8 hours.

Serves 6

Cooking time: 6–8 hours
Preparation time: 30 minutes
Attention: Minimal
Pot size: 3–5 quarts

3 pounds beef brisket
½ teaspoon seasoning salt
¾ cup brown sugar
1 onion
1 can beer

Caper Pork

Cooking time: 7–9 hours
Preparation time: 30 minutes
Attention: Minimal
Pot size: 3–5 quarts

2 pounds pork
2 tablespoons olive oil
1 onion
4 stalks celery
2 carrots
3 cloves garlic
1 cup tomato sauce
6 black olives
¼ cup dry white wine
1 tablespoon capers

Here is your opportunity to use capers in your cooking.
The capers in this recipe give the pork a refreshing zing.

1. Cut the meat into serving-size pieces. Sauté in the olive oil in a pan over medium heat until the meat is lightly browned. Set the meat aside, leaving the meat juices in the pan.

2. Cut the onion, celery, and carrots into ½-inch slices. Mince the garlic. Use the same pan to heat the vegetables and garlic over high heat for 5 minutes.

3. Transfer the vegetable mix, then the meat, to the slow cooker. Pour the tomato sauce over the meat.

4. Cover and heat on a low setting for 6 to 8 hours.

5. Quarter the olives. Half an hour before serving, add the olives, wine, and capers (with caper juice) to the slow cooker.

The Right Olives

Just say no to pimento-stuffed green olives. Go to a Middle Eastern grocery and buy an olive sampler. Try the giant black olives and the small wrinkled ones. There are olives available you didn't know existed. Once you taste them, you'll forsake the pimento-stuffed versions in jars, and use these in your cooking instead.

Flamed Beef

Be sure to use caution when flaming the meat!
You can serve this dish with hot and buttery wide egg noodles.

Serves 6

Cooking time: 5–7 hours
Preparation time: 30 minutes
Attention: Minimal
Pot size: 3–5 quarts

4 slices bacon
2½ pounds beef chuck
¼ cup flour
1 teaspoon salt
½ teaspoon pepper
¼ cup brandy
2 cloves garlic
1 onion
1 teaspoon thyme
¼ teaspoon marjoram
¼ teaspoon sage
½ cup water
1¾ cups burgundy
½ pound mushrooms

1. Sauté the bacon in a pan over medium heat until crisp. Set aside the bacon slices, leaving the bacon drippings in the pan.

2. Cube the beef. Combine the flour, salt, and pepper. Roll the beef cubes in the flour mixture. Sauté in the bacon drippings in the pan over medium heat until lightly browned. Drain the meat; transfer the browned beef cubes to the slow cooker.

3. Warm the brandy in a saucepan over medium heat until it steams, then pour the brandy over the meat in the slow cooker and light it.

4. Mince the garlic and dice the onion. Add the garlic, onion, herbs, water, and half of the burgundy to the slow cooker after the flame is extinguished. Cover and heat on a low setting for 4 to 6 hours.

5. Slice the mushrooms. An hour before serving add the mushrooms and the remaining burgundy.

Be Tough and Tender

You can save money without your guests even knowing by getting tougher cuts of meat. You'll just have to spend more time tenderizing. If your chosen recipe doesn't already call for vinegar, add a tablespoon or two to the cooking broth and the meat will be tender in no time.

Peking Gin Roast

Don't be alarmed by the coffee and gin in this recipe.
They add a nice rich flavor to the meat.

Serves 10

Cooking time: 6–8 hours
Preparation time: 30 minutes
Attention: Minimal
Pot size: 3–5 quarts

1 onion
5 pounds beef roast
1 cup vinegar
2 tablespoons oil
2 cups black coffee
1 cup water
½ teaspoon salt
¼ teaspoon pepper
½ cup gin

1. Slice the onion. Cut the meat into serving-size pieces and mix with the onion slices. Put the meat mixture in a glass dish and cover with the vinegar. Refrigerate for 24 to 48 hours, then discard the vinegar.

2. Sauté the meat and onions in oil in a pan over high heat until the meat is browned. Transfer the mixture to the slow cooker.

3. Pour the coffee and water over the meat and onions.

4. Cover and heat on a low setting for 6 to 8 hours.

5. Half an hour before serving, add the salt, pepper, and gin.

Looking at Liquids
When adapting recipes for use in a slow cooker, cut the amount of liquids in half, or more if "wet" ingredients (like tomatoes) are used. Very little evaporation takes place in a slow cooker because it is self-contained and sealed.

Sweet and Sour Pork

Serve this dish with rice, preferably stir-fried with some eggs,
sliced green onion, and a dash of soy sauce.

Serves 6

Cooking time: 6–8 hours
Preparation time: 30 minutes
Attention: Minimal
Pot size: 3–5 quarts

1. Cube the pork. Sauté the pork in oil in a pan over medium heat until lightly browned.

2. Cube the pineapple. Transfer the pork and pineapple to the slow cooker, mixing them well.

3. Dissolve the cornstarch in the water in a mixing bowl. Add the vinegar, sugar, salt, soy sauce, and pineapple juice. Pour over the meat mixture.

4. Cover and heat on a low setting for 6 to 8 hours.

5. Thinly slice the green pepper and onion. Half an hour before serving, stir in the green pepper and onion.

3 pounds pork
1 tablespoon oil
1 pound fresh pineapple
4 tablespoons cornstarch
1 cup water
⅔ cup vinegar
½ cup brown sugar
1 teaspoon salt
2 tablespoons soy sauce
2 cups pineapple juice
1 green pepper
1 onion

Savory Beef Stroganoff

This dish is best prepared the day before, and left overnight in the refrigerator. Then reheat and serve over egg noodles with poppy seeds.

Serves 6

Cooking time: 6–8 hours
Preparation time: 30 minutes
Attention: Moderate
Pot size: 3–5 quarts

1 clove garlic
2 stalks celery
1 onion
1 pound mushrooms
2 tablespoons butter
2 pounds beef steak
3 tablespoons flour
2 tablespoons butter
2 tablespoons catsup
2 tablespoons sherry
1 cup beef broth
1 tablespoon Worcestershire
    sauce
1 small bunch parsley
½ cup sour cream

1. Mince the garlic and slice the celery. Transfer to the slow cooker. Slice the onion and mushrooms. Sauté in butter in a pan over medium heat until the onions are soft. Set aside the mushroom mixture but keep the juices in the pan.

2. Slice the meat into ¼-inch strips. Coat with the flour, and sauté in the pan with the mushroom juices, plus an additional 2 tablespoons butter, until lightly browned. Mix the onion and meat mixtures together as they are transferred to the slow cooker.

3. Mix the catsup, sherry, broth, and Worcestershire sauce in a small bowl. Pour the mixture into the slow cooker. Cover and heat on a low setting for 6 to 8 hours.

4. Let stand overnight in the refrigerator.

5. Reheat the mixture. Mince the parsley. Half an hour before serving, stir in the sour cream and parsley.

Browning Meats

Browning meats for ten minutes or so before putting them in the slow cooker makes them come out more tender at the end. They also get that nice seared look, adding to the visual appeal of your dish.

chapter 9
seafood and poultry

Hot Chili Crab Soup

This soup will require cold beverages to clear the palate before the next dish.
Be sure to have mild lemonade and sparkling water on hand.

Serves 6

Cooking time: 2–3 hours
Preparation time: 60 minutes
Attention: Minimal
Pot size: 3–5 quarts

3 cloves garlic
½ jalapeno pepper
1 onion
1 tablespoon vegetable oil
2 pounds Italian plum
 tomatoes
4 cups chicken broth
1 cup tomato sauce
2 teaspoons chili powder
2 teaspoons cumin
¼ teaspoon salt
3 tablespoons lime juice
1½ cups corn kernels
½ pound crabmeat
10 corn tortillas
1 bunch cilantro
1 avocado
½ pound Cheddar cheese
1 lime
1 jalapeno pepper

1. Finely mince the garlic and ½ jalapeno, and chop the onion. Sauté the onion, garlic, and jalapeno in the oil in a pan over low heat until the onion is soft.

2. Chop the tomatoes. Put the onion mixture, tomatoes, broth, tomato sauce, spices, salt, lime juice, and corn in the slow cooker.

3. Cover and heat on a low setting for 2 to 3 hours.

4. Shred the crabmeat. Before serving, stir in the crabmeat.

5. Prepare the garnishes as follows: Slice the tortillas into strips and brown on a baking sheet in a 300°F oven. Chop the cilantro, slice the avocado, shred the cheese, slice the lime, and mince the jalapeno. Serve in separate dishes near the slow cooker.

Hot Stuff

Chili pepper "heat" varies dramatically by species. Typically, the small, pointed chilies are the hottest, while large, blunt chilies (those that look more like bell peppers) are the mildest. Also, fresh chilies are hotter than dried ones, so beware!

Fillet of Sole with Grapes and White Wine

*Fillet of sole is a delicate fish, and this dish is nice and mild.
Serve with Savory Rye Berries (page 68) for dramatic contrast.*

Serves 6

Cooking time: 2–3 hours
Preparation time: 60 minutes
Attention: Minimal
Pot size: 3–5 quarts

¼ pound mushrooms
½ pound seedless grapes
2 white onions
2 tablespoons butter
4 tablespoons butter
4 tablespoons flour
¼ teaspoon salt
¼ teaspoon pepper
1 cup milk
2 cups cream
1 cup white wine
3 pounds fillet of sole
¼ cup buttered toast crumbs

1. Quarter the mushrooms, halve the grapes, and finely slice the onions. Sauté mushrooms, grapes, and onions in 2 tablespoons butter in a pan over low heat until the onions are soft. Set aside the mushroom mixture, retaining the juices in the pan.

2. Add the remaining butter to the pan and melt. Mix the flour in slowly, then the salt, pepper, milk, and cream. Let thicken over low heat. Remove from the heat and stir in the wine.

3. Layer the mushroom mixture, fillets, and cream sauce in the slow cooker.

4. Cover and heat on a low setting for 2 to 3 hours.

5. Before serving, sprinkle the buttered crumbs over the top as a garnish.

Something's Fishy

To get rid of that fishy taste soak fish in vinegar and water before cooking. This will make it sweet and tender. Test it out by soaking one fillet and not soaking another, then lightly broiling without adding spices. How do they compare?

Chef's Fish Broth

Keep a resealable container in the freezer for miscellaneous fish bones.
When you have enough, make a broth just like the chefs do.

Makes about 4 cups

Cooking time: 3–4 hours
Preparation time: 15 minutes
Attention: Minimal
Pot size: 3–5 quarts

1 onion
1 carrot
3 cups fish bones
3 cups water
1 bouquet garni
1 cup white wine

1. Coarsely chop the onion and carrot. Add the onion, carrot, bones, water, bouquet garni, and wine to the slow cooker.

2. Cover and heat on a low setting for 3 to 4 hours.

3. Strain and use in soups, chowders, or sauces, or freeze.

Pasta with Cheese and Oysters

This is not the macaroni and cheese you ate as a kid.
Oysters give this dish party appeal and a delicious twist.

Serves 8

Cooking time: 3–4 hours
Preparation time: 45 minutes
Attention: Minimal
Pot size: 3–5 quarts

½ cup butter
½ pound Colby cheese
1 pound uncooked macaroni
½ pound salted oyster
*   crackers*
½ pound oyster meats
6 cups milk

1. Butter the inside of the slow cooker with half of the butter.

2. Shred the cheese. Make several layers each of the macaroni, cheese, crackers, and oysters in the slow cooker. Pour the milk over the layers and dot with the remaining butter. Cover and heat on a low setting for 3 to 4 hours.

Seafood and Sherry Chowder

Serve this with toasted slices of Classic Brown Bread (page 54)
for a nice contrast in colors and textures.

Serves 6

Cooking time: 3–4 hours
Preparation time: 45 minutes
Attention: Minimal
Pot size: 3–5 quarts

1 onion
4 stalks celery
¼ pound mushrooms
3 tablespoons butter
3 tablespoons flour
3 cups milk
½ pound lobster meat
½ pound shrimp
1 cup cream
2 tablespoons parsley
¼ cup dry sherry

1. Chop the onion, celery, and mushrooms; sauté in butter in a pan over medium heat until the onions are soft.

2. Blend the flour into the melted butter, then add 1 cup of the milk and stir over low heat until the sauce is smooth and thickened.

3. Shred the lobster meat. Clean and devein shrimp. Transfer the onion mixture, remaining milk, cream, and seafood to the slow cooker.

4. Cover and heat on a low setting for 2 to 3 hours.

5. Chop the parsley. Half an hour before serving, stir in the sherry and the parsley.

Sweeten Your Shrimp

Soak canned shrimp in a teaspoon of sherry and 2 tablespoons of vinegar for 15 minutes. This will eliminate that metallic taste and make them sweet and delicious, as if you caught them yourself that very morning.

Tomato Shrimp Supreme

Provide your guests with soft white bread or
hunks of a crunchy baguette to soak up the juices of this dish.

Serves 6

Cooking time: 2–3 hours
Preparation time: 45 minutes
Attention: Minimal
Pot size: 3–5 quarts

1 pound mushrooms
½ green bell pepper
½ onion
2 tablespoons butter
1 tablespoon flour
¼ teaspoon salt
¼ teaspoon pepper
¼ teaspoon cayenne pepper
6 tomatoes
6 stalks celery
1 teaspoon sugar
1 pound shrimp, peeled and
    deveined
1 cup white wine

1. Quarter the mushrooms; chop the green pepper and onion.

2. Sauté the mushrooms, green pepper, and onion in butter in a pan over low heat until the onion is soft. Add the flour, salt, pepper, and cayenne pepper to the mushroom mixture; stir over low heat until the sauce thickens.

3. Transfer to the slow cooker.

4. Coarsely chop the tomatoes and thinly slice the celery. Add the tomatoes, celery, sugar, and shrimp to the slow cooker.

5. Cover and heat on a low setting for 2 to 3 hours.

6. Half an hour before serving, add the wine.

Pimento Shrimp Pot

This is a good all-in-one dish with lots of color.
Add fresh cilantro as a garnish, or fresh mint if cilantro isn't available.

Serves 8

Cooking time: 2–3 hours
Preparation time: 45 minutes
Attention: Minimal
Pot size: 3–5 quarts

1. Quarter the mushrooms; sauté in butter in a pan over medium heat until lightly browned.

2. Cut the pimento into thin strips.

3. Add the mushrooms, green pepper, celery, tomatoes, pimento, shrimp, rice, salt, and chili powder to the slow cooker.

4. Cover and heat on a low setting for 2 to 3 hours.

1 pound mushrooms
¼ cup butter
2 ounces pimento
1 cup chopped green pepper
1 cup finely sliced celery
2½ cups coarsely chopped tomatoes
2 pounds shrimp, peeled and deveined
2 cups cooked rice
1 teaspoon salt
½ teaspoon chili powder

Delta Shrimp

*Shrimp come in several different sizes. For some visual variety,
try using more than one size in your shrimp dishes.*

Serves 4

Cooking time: 2–3 hours
Preparation time: 45 minutes
Attention: Minimal
Pot size: 3–5 quarts

2 onions
1 cup chopped celery
2 tablespoons butter
1 tablespoon flour
1 teaspoon salt
1 cup water
4 tomatoes
1 green pepper
1 tablespoon vinegar
2 tablespoons chili powder
1 teaspoon sugar
1 pound shrimp, peeled and
    deveined

1. Slice the onions. Sauté the onions with the chopped celery in butter in a pan over medium heat until the onion is soft. Add the flour and salt; stir to thicken. Add the water slowly and mix well.

2. Coarsely chop the tomatoes and green pepper. Transfer the onion mixture, tomatoes, green pepper, vinegar, chili powder, and sugar to the slow cooker.

3. Cover and heat on a low setting for 2 to 3 hours.

4. Half an hour before serving, add the shrimp.

Silky Shrimp Soup

Use fresh shrimp, if possible. The fresh shrimp shells add a little extra flavor while cooking, so leave them on until the end.

Serves 6

Cooking time: 2–3 hours
Preparation time: 30 minutes
Attention: Moderate
Pot size: 3–5 quarts

1 clove garlic
1 onion
1½ pounds shrimp
4 cups fish stock
½ teaspoon thyme
½ teaspoon black pepper
1 cup heavy cream
¼ cup dry sherry

1. Finely chop the garlic and onion. Put the garlic, onion, and shrimp into the slow cooker with the stock and spices.

2. Cover and heat on a low setting for 2 to 3 hours.

3. Half an hour before serving, remove the shrimp from the broth using a slotted spoon. Shell the shrimp and discard the shells.

4. Puree half of the shrimp meats with the cream. Add the whole shrimp, the pureed shrimp mixture, and the sherry to the broth in the slow cooker.

Tented Tilapia

*For extra flavor, add some fresh basil or
mint leaves to the tents before heating in the slow cooker.*

Serves 6–8

Cooking time: 1–2 hours
Preparation time: 15 minutes
Attention: Minimal
Pot size: 3–5 quarts

3 cloves garlic
2 tomatoes
2 pounds tilapia fillets
½ teaspoon seasoned salt
¼ cup butter
1 cup white wine

1. Mince the garlic and thinly slice the tomatoes. Lay each fillet in a rectangle of aluminum foil large enough to fold over and seal. Put this on each fillet: seasoned salt, dabs of butter, garlic, tomato, wine. Seal packages.

3. Arrange the wrapped fish on a trivet or rack in the slow cooker. Pour water around the base of the trivet. Cover and heat on high setting for 1 to 2 hours.

Easy BBQ Chicken Dinner

*You can dress up this simple dish by making your own barbecue sauce.
Try Smoky Barbecue Sauce (page 49).*

Serves 4–6

Cooking time: 3–4 hours
Preparation time: 15 minutes
Attention: Minimal
Pot size: 3–5 quarts

1 onion
1 pound baby red potatoes
1 pound mushrooms
2 pounds chicken breasts
1½ cups barbecue sauce

1. Thinly slice the onion and potatoes; halve the mushrooms. Arrange in the slow cooker in that order; lay the chicken on top. Cover with barbecue sauce.

2. Cover and heat on a low setting for 3 to 4 hours.

Chili Beer Chicken

This is definitely a safe bet for a Super Bowl party,
but it is also a tasty addition to a holiday buffet.

1. Cut the chicken into serving-size pieces. Coat the chicken pieces in a mixture of the flour, ½ teaspoon salt, and pepper.

2. Slice the onions. Sauté the chicken pieces and half of the sliced onions in butter in a pan over medium heat until the chicken is browned.

3. Arrange the chicken mixture and the remaining uncooked onion in the slow cooker.

4. Mix the beer, tomato sauce, chili powder, and remaining salt in a bowl; pour the mixture over the chicken and onions.

5. Cover and heat on a low setting for 3 to 4 hours.

Variations in Chicken

The taste of chicken, as well as the taste of beef and pork, reflects the diet of the animal. Did it keep a standard diet or did it consume a variety of wild foods with lots of exotic flavors? Pay attention to where your meat was raised and how it was treated.

Serves 6

Cooking time: 3–4 hours
Preparation time: 45 minutes
Attention: Minimal
Pot size: 3–5 quarts

3 pounds chicken
½ cup flour
½ teaspoon salt
½ teaspoon pepper
2 onions
6 tablespoons butter
1 bottle beer
1 cup tomato sauce
½ teaspoon chili powder
½ teaspoon salt

Chicken Cacciatore

*Serve this classic dish with wild rice, egg noodles,
or small pumpernickel rolls to soak up the sauce.*

Serves 6

Cooking time: 4–5 hours
Preparation time: 45 minutes
Attention: Minimal
Pot size: 3–5 quarts

3 pounds chicken
1 onion
½ cup olive oil
1 clove garlic
5 tomatoes
½ teaspoon salt
¼ teaspoon pepper
1 cup chicken broth
½ cup white wine

1. Cut the chicken into serving-size pieces. Slice the onion. Sauté the chicken pieces and onion in olive oil in a pan over medium heat until the chicken is browned.

2. Crush the garlic. Coarsely chop the garlic and tomatoes.

3. Combine the chicken mixture, garlic, and tomatoes in the slow cooker. Sprinkle with the salt and pepper; add the broth.

4. Cover and heat on low setting for 3 to 4 hours.

5. Half an hour before serving, add the wine.

Nice Rice

If you don't have a rice cooker, use a slow cooker as your kitchen assistant. Slow cookers do a great job of keeping rice warm without overcooking it. This can be very handy for party preparation when you've got a full day planned, or want time for a nap.

Tamales with Chicken and Olives

You can buy tamales fresh, frozen, or bottled, but they're much better made from scratch. Try the recipe for Homemade Tamales (page 33).

1. Melt the butter in a saucepan over low heat; add the flour and stir to blend and thicken. Blend in the chicken broth and mix until smooth over low heat.

2. Mince the olives and cube the chicken meat. Add the olives, chicken, tomato puree, corn, raisins, salt, and chili powder to the thickened chicken sauce.

3. Remove the husks from the tamales and arrange the tamales in the slow cooker. Top each layer of tamales with sauce and cheese.

4. Cover and heat on a low setting for 3 to 4 hours.

Handle Dairy with Care

Recipes including fresh milk, cream, or cheese may require the dairy product to be added only at or near the end. Extended periods of cooking can cause dairy products to separate. An acidic broth, such as a tomato-based one, can have a similar effect.

Serves 6

Cooking time: 3–4 hours
Preparation time: 45 minutes
Attention: Minimal
Pot size: 3–5 quarts

1 tablespoon butter
1 tablespoon flour
1 cup chicken broth
1 cup olives, pitted
1 pound boneless chicken
    meat
1 cup tomato puree
1 cup corn
¼ cup raisins
½ teaspoon salt
2 teaspoons chili powder
8 large tamales (or 16 small)
½ cup shredded Monterey
    Jack cheese

Cinnamon Chicken Pasta

*Cinnamon and chicken aren't commonly combined,
but they work together perfectly in this recipe.*

Serves 6

Cooking time: 4–5 hours
Preparation time: 45 minutes
Attention: Minimal
Pot size: 3–5 quarts

3 pounds chicken
½ teaspoon salt
½ teaspoon pepper
½ lemon
½ cup olive oil
6 ounces tomato paste
1 cup water
1 stick cinnamon bark
4 cups cooked pasta, firm

1. Cut the chicken into serving-size pieces. Roll the chicken pieces in salt and pepper, then drizzle with the juice from the ½ lemon. Sauté the chicken pieces in olive oil in a pan over medium heat until lightly browned. Transfer the chicken to a slow cooker, but retain the juices in the pan.

2. Add the tomato paste, water, and cinnamon stick to the same pan and stir over low heat until well mixed with the chicken juices.

3. Pour the tomato mixture over the chicken in the slow cooker.

4. Cover and heat on a low setting for 3 to 4 hours.

5. Half an hour before serving, stir the pasta into the sauce. Remove cinnamon stick before serving, if not completely dissolved.

Fresh Herbs

These can be expensive and sometimes they're not even available. Solution? Grow your own or buy them in season, blanch quickly, chill, dry, seal, and freeze. Then enjoy herbs all year, just taking what you need out of the freezer.

White Pasta Sauce with Chicken

*Use fresh Parmesan or Romano cheese, grated from a block,
instead of the packaged kind. Serve with fresh pasta.*

1. Cube the chicken; sauté in olive oil in a pan over medium heat until the chicken is browned. Set aside the chicken pieces. Retain the chicken juices in the pan.

2. Crush the garlic. Coarsely chop the garlic, green pepper, and mushrooms. Slice the pimento into thin strips. Sauté the garlic, green pepper, mushrooms, and pimento in the juices and oil remaining from the chicken. Add the flour and stir over low heat to blend and thicken. Add the chicken broth and stir over low heat until smooth. Remove from heat and add the salt, pepper, and Worcestershire sauce.

3. Thinly slice the celery. Put half of the celery in the slow cooker, then the chicken, half of the mushroom mixture, the remainder of the celery, and the remainder of the mushroom mixture.

4. Cover and heat on a low setting for 3 to 4 hours.

5. Grate the cheese and provide as a garnish.

Cooking time: 3–4 hours
Preparation time: 60 minutes
Attention: Minimal
Pot size: 3–5 quarts

3 pounds boneless, skinless chicken
2 tablespoons olive oil
2 cloves garlic
1 green pepper
½ pound mushrooms
4 ounces pimento
2 tablespoons flour
1½ cups chicken broth
½ teaspoon salt
¼ teaspoon pepper
2 tablespoons Worcestershire sauce
6 stalks celery
¼ pound Parmesan cheese

Country Brunch Eggs

Save your stale bread of all kinds for this dish.
The drier the bread, the more of the egg mixture it will soak up.

Serves 6

Cooking time: 2–3 hours
Preparation time: 45 minutes
Attention: Minimal
Pot size: 3–5 quarts

1 pound bulk sausage
6 eggs
¼ teaspoon salt
1 teaspoon dry mustard
2 cups milk
½ pound Cheddar cheese
6 slices bread
2 tablespoons butter

1. Crumble and sauté the sausage in a pan over medium heat until browned, then drain.

2. Beat the eggs. Add the salt, mustard, and milk to the eggs and mix well.

3. Shred the cheese and cube the bread.

4. Butter the inside of the slow cooker. Put the bread and sausage in the slow cooker and sprinkle with the cheese. Pour the egg mixture carefully over the top.

5. Cover and heat on a low setting for 2 to 3 hours.

Slumber Party

If your child has a slumber party, let the guests make their own fruit mix in the evening, to slowly steep overnight and yield a special pancake or cereal topping in the morning. You can also dribble some stewed fruit right over the pancake batter as it cooks, locking it right into the pancake.

chapter 10
wild game

Bing Cherry Pheasant

*Cherries have a rich, savory taste that is especially delicious
when coupled with a buttery pheasant.*

Serves 8

Cooking time: 4–6 hours
Preparation time: 60 minutes
Attention: Minimal
Pot size: 3–5 quarts

4 pounds pheasant
½ teaspoon salt
½ teaspoon pepper
2 tablespoons flour
¼ cup butter
1 pound fresh Bing cherries
1 cup red wine
6 whole cloves
½ cup water
½ cup sugar
1 cup cream

1. Cut the pheasant into serving-size pieces. Combine the salt, pepper, and flour. Roll the pheasant pieces in the flour mixture; sauté in butter in a pan over medium heat until browned. Transfer to the slow cooker.

2. Pit and halve the cherries. Add half of the cherries, half of the wine, the cloves, and the water to the slow cooker. Cover and heat on a low setting for 4 to 6 hours.

3. Mix the sugar, remaining cherries, and remaining wine in a saucepan over low heat; stir until partly reduced.

4. An hour before serving, add the cream to the slow cooker.

5. When serving, provide the reduced cherry mixture as a sauce.

Pheasant with Orange

This goes well with Orange Raisin Bread (page 59), or you can cream some orange pulp into a soft spread and serve it with crusty French bread.

1. Cut the pheasant into serving-size pieces and remove the skin. Shake the pieces in flour, salt, and pepper to coat; sauté in butter and olive oil in a pan over medium heat until browned. Transfer to the slow cooker.

2. Add the orange juice and raisins to the meat.

3. Cover and heat on a low setting for 4 to 6 hours.

4. Coarsely chop the rosemary and parsley. Half an hour before serving, add the herbs and wine to the slow cooker.

Serves 6

Cooking time: 4–6 hours
Preparation time: 45 minutes
Attention: Minimal
Pot size: 3–5 quarts

3 pounds pheasant
⅔ cup flour
½ teaspoon salt
¼ teaspoon pepper
2 tablespoons butter
2 tablespoons olive oil
1 cup orange juice
½ cup white raisins
2–4 sprigs fresh rosemary
1 small bunch fresh parsley
1 cup white wine

Pheasant with Sauerkraut

Pheasant can be very dry, but the sauerkraut in this recipe keeps the meat moist and tender.

1. Cut the pheasant meat into serving-size pieces; thinly slice the onion. Sauté the meat and onion in oil in a pan over medium heat until lightly browned.

2. Drain the sauerkraut. Layer the meat, sauerkraut, and spices in the slow cooker. Pour the beer over the top.

3. Cover and heat on a low setting for 4 to 6 hours. Remove bay leaves before serving.

Serves 4–6

Cooking time: 4–6 hours
Preparation time: 30 minutes
Attention: Minimal
Pot size: 3–5 quarts

2 pounds pheasant
1 onion
2 tablespoons vegetable oil
2 pounds sauerkraut
2 bay leaves
6 cloves
16 ounces beer

Reindeer Stew

Reindeer is actually domesticated caribou. This recipe can also be made with venison if you don't have any reindeer on hand.

Serves 10–12

Cooking time: 4–6 hours
Preparation time: 60 minutes
Attention: Minimal
Pot size: 3–5 quarts

1 pound baby potatoes
1 pound mushrooms
2 tablespoons olive oil
5 pounds reindeer
½ teaspoon salt
½ teaspoon pepper
¼ cup butter
¼ cup flour
1 cup water
2 cups red wine
1 bouquet garni

1. Halve the baby potatoes and mushrooms. Sauté them in oil in a pan over medium heat until the mushrooms are slightly browned. Transfer to the slow cooker.

2. Cube the meat. Roll in the salt and pepper, then sauté in the butter in a pan over medium heat until lightly browned. Add the flour and stir over medium heat until the flour browns, then stir in the water and mix while the sauce thickens. Transfer the meat and sauce to the slow cooker.

3. Add the wine and bouquet garni to the meat.

4. Cover and heat on a low setting for 4 to 6 hours.

Cinnamon Apple Pheasant

Use good baking apples, like Rome or Granny Smith, for some extra tartness. You can leave the peels on for a little more color.

Serves 8

Cooking time: 4–6 hours
Preparation time: 30 minutes
Attention: Minimal
Pot size: 3–5 quarts

4 pounds pheasant
½ teaspoon salt
½ teaspoon black pepper
¼ cup butter
4 apples
2 cups apple cider
2 sticks cinnamon bark

1. Cut the pheasant into serving-size pieces and roll in the salt and pepper. Sauté in butter in a pan over medium heat until lightly browned.

2. Core and slice the apples. Layer the pheasant with the apple slices in the slow cooker. Add the cider and cinnamon.

3. Cover and heat on a low setting for 4 to 6 hours.

Country Hare Stew

*This recipe takes some advance planning, but it's a sure way
to impress your guests. Serve this with small black bread rolls.*

Serves 4–6

Cooking time: 6–8 hours
Preparation time: 90 minutes
Attention: Moderate
Pot size: 3–5 quarts

2 pounds rabbit
1 carrot
1 onion
1 cup white wine
1 cup water
1 bouquet garni
*1 teaspoon whole black
    peppercorns*
½ pound butter
2 tablespoons flour
1 cup water
¼ pound salt pork
10 pearl onions
½ pound mushrooms
*1 tablespoon chopped
    parsley*

1. Cut the rabbit meat into pieces. Scrub, peel, and chop the carrot and peel and chop the onion. Marinate the meat in the refrigerator with the carrot, onion, wine, 1 cup water, bouquet garni, and peppercorns. After 2 days, remove the meat; strain the marinade and save the juice, discarding the vegetables and spices.

2. Melt the butter in a pan over medium heat and mix in the flour until blended. Add the marinated meat, stir for a few minutes, then slowly stir in the strained marinade and the remaining 1 cup of water. Transfer to the slow cooker. Cover and heat on a low setting for 4 to 6 hours.

3. Cube the salt pork and peel the onions. Heat the pork with the onions in water in a covered pot over high heat until boiling; drain and discard the liquid.

4. Halve the mushrooms. Sauté the boiled pork, boiled onions, and mushrooms in a pan over medium heat until the pork is browned. Drain, then transfer to the slow cooker with the meat.

5. Cover the slow cooker and heat on a low setting another 2 hours. Before serving, stir in the parsley.

Too Salty?

If your soup is too salty, put a piece of raw potato in the soup or add a spoonful each of cider vinegar and sugar. If soup is too greasy, drop in a lettuce leaf, then take it back out after two minutes. The leaf will take some grease along with it.

Hungarian Rabbit

Serves 8

Cooking time: 4–6 hours
Preparation time: 60 minutes
Attention: Minimal
Pot size: 3–5 quarts

1 egg
1 teaspoon milk
4 pounds rabbit
⅓ cup flour
1 tablespoon paprika
½ teaspoon salt
¼ teaspoon pepper
2 onions
3 tablespoons butter
1 cup white wine
¼ cup water
1 cup sour cream
2 teaspoons paprika

Rabbit and paprika are a delicious combination.
This dish goes well with fresh sourdough bread or Tangy Rice (page 67).

1. Beat the egg and milk together.

2. Cut the rabbit meat into pieces. Dip the pieces in the egg mixture, then coat the pieces by shaking them in a mixture of the flour, 1 tablespoon paprika, salt, and pepper.

3. Thinly slice the onions. Sauté the meat and onions in butter in a pan over medium heat until the meat is lightly browned. Transfer the meat and onions to the slow cooker. Add the wine and water.

4. Cover and heat on a low setting for 4 to 6 hours.

5. Half an hour before serving, add the sour cream and remaining 2 teaspoons paprika to the slow cooker.

Rainbow of Olives

Not all olives are green, and those little red pimentos are optional. Try wrinkly black Turkish olives or giant green olives. Make olive paste to use as a sandwich garnish, or throw a handful of olive slices in your soup.

Wild Duck Gumbo

You can substitute other dark, rich wild fowl for duck in this recipe.
Serve with wild rice, barley, or polenta.

1. Cut the duck into serving-size pieces. Roll the pieces in the salt and pepper and sprinkle with Tabasco. Sauté the duck in the oil in a pan over medium heat until the meat is browned, then transfer to the slow cooker.

2. Melt the butter in a pan over low heat. Blend in the flour and stir until lightly browned.

3. Mince the onion and garlic. Add to the browned flour mixture and stir over low heat until the onion is soft.

4. Add the onion mixture and water to the slow cooker. Cover and heat on a low setting for 4 to 5 hours.

5. Half an hour before serving, take out the pieces of duck and remove the bones, then put the meat back in the slow cooker. Add the oysters and oyster liquor.

Go for the Garlic

Garlic is good added just before serving a dish. It has a whole different flavor than garlic that has been cooking for a while. Depending on the tastes of your guests, you can mince it finely or leave it in large, coarse pieces.

Serves 6

Cooking time: 4–5 hours
Preparation time: 60 minutes
Attention: Moderate
Pot size: 3–5 quarts

3 pounds duck
1½ teaspoons salt
1 teaspoon black pepper
½ teaspoon Tabasco sauce
¼ cup oil
3 tablespoons butter
3 tablespoons flour
1 onion
4 cloves garlic
6 cups water
2 dozen oysters, with liquor

Campfire Duck

Fresh duck should hang to age for about six days in the cold before cooking.
Ask a butcher or hunter for help with this.

Serves 6–8

Cooking time: 4–6 hours
Preparation time: 30 minutes
Attention: Minimal
Pot size: 3–5 quarts

3 pounds duck, aged
1 teaspoon seasoning salt
½ cup flour
4 slices bacon
½ cup water
½ cup heavy cream

1. Cut the meat into serving-size pieces. Rub with the salt and roll in the flour. Mince the bacon. Sauté the duck and bacon in a pan over high heat until browned. Adjust the heat to low. Stir in the water and mix to thicken.

2. Transfer the meat and juices to the slow cooker. Cover and heat on low setting for 4 to 6 hours. Half an hour before serving, stir in the cream.

Venison with Gingered Sauerkraut

Serve big, buttery pumpernickel croutons with this dish.
Cube the bread, dunk in melted butter, sprinkle with herbs, and toast.

Serves 4–6

Cooking time: 4–6 hours
Preparation time: 30 minutes
Attention: Minimal
Pot size: 3–5 quarts

2 pounds venison
1 pound mushrooms
2 tablespoons vegetable oil
1 onion
1½ pounds sauerkraut
½ cup water
2 tablespoons brown sugar
½ cup red wine vinegar
1 teaspoon soy sauce
½ teaspoon ground ginger

1. Cube the meat and quarter the mushrooms. Sauté meat and mushrooms in oil in a pan over medium heat until the meat is lightly browned.

2. Thinly slice the onion. Drain the sauerkraut. Mix the water, sugar, vinegar, soy sauce, and ginger in a small mixing bowl.

3. Layer the meat mixture, onion, and sauerkraut in the slow cooker. Pour the vinegar mixture over the top.

4. Cover and heat on a low setting for 4 to 6 hours.

Hot BBQ Squirrel

*If you don't have squirrel, you could substitute chicken or pork.
But if you can get squirrel meat, give it a try.*

1. Cut the squirrel meat into pieces. Cut the bacon into 1-inch pieces, and crush the garlic.

2. Sauté the meat, bacon, and garlic in a pan over medium heat until the meat is lightly browned. Transfer to the slow cooker.

3. Add the catsup, water, sugar, and Worcestershire sauce.

4. Cover and heat on low setting for 4 to 6 hours.

5. An hour before serving, add the chili powder and pepper sauce.

Serves 8–10

Cooking time: 5–7 hours
Preparation time: 30 minutes
Attention: Minimal
Pot size: 3–5 quarts

4 pounds squirrel
2 slices bacon
1 clove garlic
1 cup catsup
½ cup water
½ cup brown sugar
⅓ cup Worcestershire sauce
1 teaspoon chili powder
3 drops red pepper sauce

Pepper Duck

*This goes well with fresh whole wheat bread, or sections of
whole wheat pita loaves. Also, use wild mushrooms, if possible.*

1. Remove the bones and skin from the duck; cube the meat. Shake the meat in flour, salt, and pepper to coat. Thinly slice the onion and halve the mushrooms.

2. Sauté the duck, onion, and mushrooms in butter in a pan over medium heat until the duck is lightly browned. Put the duck mixture, water, wine, and bay leaves in the slow cooker.

3. Cover and heat on low setting for 4 to 6 hours.

4. Mince the green pepper, and add half an hour before serving.

Serves 6–8

Cooking time: 4–6 hours
Preparation time: 30 minutes
Attention: Minimal
Pot size: 3–5 quarts

3 pounds duck
½ cup flour
1 teaspoon salt
1 teaspoon pepper
1 onion
½ pound mushrooms
¼ cup butter
1 cup water
½ cup dry red wine
2 bay leaves
1 green pepper

Dove with Herbs

Dove has a dark, rich flavor. Complement this by providing your guests with mild sides like Parsley Almond Rice (page 52) or fresh cherries.

1. Chop the onion and slice the mushrooms. Sauté the onion and mushrooms in butter in a pan over medium heat until the onion is soft. Add the dove and sauté over medium heat until the meat is lightly browned.

2. Transfer the meat and vegetables to the slow cooker, leaving the juices in the pan. Add the flour to the pan. Stir over low heat to blend and thicken, then mix in the water. Transfer to the slow cooker with half the wine.

3. Cover and heat on low setting for 4 to 6 hours.

4. Coarsely chop the herbs. Half an hour before serving, add the herbs and the remaining wine to the slow cooker.

Cleaning Wild Game
Check your wild game carefully before cooking and remove any pellets or stones. Not even slow cooking will soften these. The pellets may be from shotgun shells, while stones may have been eaten by the animal. For example, birds do this as a digestive aid.

Sherry Duck with Dill

This goes well with Savory Rye Berries (page 68).
Use fresh dill if possible, and add it at the end for the best flavor.

Serves 4–6

Cooking time: 4–6 hours
Preparation time: 60 minutes
Attention: Minimal
Pot size: 3–5 quarts

1. Cut the meat into serving-size pieces and marinate for 24 hours, refrigerated, in the vinegar, water, oil, salt, and pepper. Strain the marinade and set aside.

2. Coat the meat with ¼ cup flour, then sauté in butter in a pan over medium heat until lightly browned. Transfer the meat to the slow cooker.

3. Add the remaining ¼ cup flour to the juices in the pan and, while heating, stir until thick. Add the marinade slowly to this and mix until smooth. Mince the olives. Add the marinade sauce, sugar, white wine, and olives to the meat in the slow cooker.

4. Cover and heat on low setting for 4 to 6 hours.

5. Coarsely chop the dill. Half an hour before serving, add the dill and sherry.

2 pounds duck
1 cup cider vinegar
½ cup water
2 tablespoons olive oil
1 teaspoon salt
¼ teaspoon pepper
¼ cup flour
3 tablespoons butter
¼ cup flour
½ cup olives
1 tablespoon sugar
½ cup white wine
2 sprigs fresh dill weed
½ cup dry sherry

Tastes of Wild Game

Wild duck can taste too wild. Let the meat soak in buttermilk overnight in the refrigerator to tame the flavor. Drain off and discard the buttermilk two hours before you start to cook.

Duck with Sauerkraut

Duck is a rich, dark meat; it goes well with the light tang of sauerkraut.
You can also substitute goose in this recipe.

Serves 8–10

Cooking time: 4–6 hours
Preparation time: 30 minutes
Attention: Minimal
Pot size: 3–5 quarts

4 pounds duck
½ teaspoon salt
½ teaspoon pepper
3 tablespoons sugar
½ cup water
8 cups sauerkraut

1. Cut the duck into serving-size pieces. Wash and dry with paper towels. Rub the meat with salt and pepper.

2. Dissolve the sugar in the water. Layer the duck and sauerkraut in the slow cooker; add the water mixture.

3. Cover and heat on a low setting for 4 to 6 hours.

Venison Roast in Orange

If you don't have access to venison, substitute beef or pork.
Use an inexpensive cut; the acidic orange juice will tenderize it during cooking.

Serves 9

Cooking time: 6–8 hours
Preparation time: 30 minutes
Attention: Moderate
Pot size: 3–5 quarts

1 slice bacon
2 cloves garlic
3 pounds venison roast
½ teaspoon salt
½ teaspoon pepper
1 bay leaf
2 whole cloves
1 cup orange juice

1. Cut the bacon into small pieces; crush and mince the garlic. Cut the meat into serving-size pieces.

2. Sauté the meat with the bacon, garlic, salt, and pepper over medium heat until the meat is lightly browned.

3. Transfer the meat and juices, bay leaf, cloves, and orange juice to the slow cooker.

4. Cover and heat on low setting for 6 to 8 hours. Open the slow cooker twice to baste, but no more.

Hassenpfeffer

*Hassenpfeffer, or "pepper rabbit" in German, is a classic rabbit dish.
Be sure to use whole peppercorns when cooking this.*

1. Cut the rabbit into serving-size pieces. Slice the onion, and crack (but do not crush) the peppercorns.

2. Marinate the rabbit in the onion, vinegar, water, salt, peppercorns, cloves, and bay leaves for 2 days, turning the meat several times. Save 1 cup of the marinade, including the onion slices and spices.

3. Sauté the meat in butter in a pan over medium heat until lightly browned; transfer to the slow cooker with the reserved 1 cup of marinade.

4. Cover and heat on a low setting for 4 to 6 hours.

5. Half an hour before serving, add the sour cream and remove the bay leaves.

Serves 6–8

Cooking time: 4–6 hours
Preparation time: 30 minutes
Attention: Minimal
Pot size: 3–5 quarts

3 pounds rabbit meat
1 onion
10 peppercorns
1½ cups vinegar
1½ cups water
½ teaspoon salt
6 cloves
2 bay leaves
3 tablespoons butter
1 cup sour cream

Elk in Wine Sauce

If a member of your family happens to hunt elk, this is a great way to use it. But if you don't have elk on hand, you can substitute beef.

Serves 6–8

Cooking time: 4–6 hours
Preparation time: 45 minutes
Attention: Minimal
Pot size: 3–5 quarts

3 pounds boneless elk roast
¼ cup flour
½ teaspoon salt
¼ teaspoon white pepper
¾ cup butter
2 onions
1 pound mushrooms
¼ pound leeks
1 cup dry wine

1. Trim the meat and cut into serving-size pieces; pat dry with a paper towel. Coat in a mixture of the flour, salt, and pepper. Sauté in half of the butter in a pan over high heat until browned. Set aside the meat, leaving the juices in the pan.

2. Finely chop the onions. Add the remaining butter to the pan and sauté the onions over medium heat until brown. Lift out the onions with a slotted spoon, leaving the juices in the pan, and transfer to the slow cooker. Put the meat over the onions.

3. Chop the mushrooms and leeks (white parts only) and add to the pan; sauté over low heat until soft, then transfer to the slow cooker.

4. Cover and heat on low setting for 4 to 6 hours.

5. Half an hour before serving, add the wine.

Name Your Foods

What's in a name? Fun! Make up wild names for your menu items. A title like "Annie's Alligator Surprise" will intrigue your guests and act as a conversation starter. Let your guests debate the ingredients for a while before disclosing the truth.

Rabbit in Coconut Sauce

The flavors of rabbit and coconut work wonderfully together in this dish.
Serve with a side of rice.

Serves 6–8

Cooking time: 4–6 hours
Preparation time: 30 minutes
Attention: Moderate
Pot size: 3–5 quarts

1 coconut
1 cup water
3 tomatoes
2 onions
1 teaspoon salt
½ teaspoon pepper
3 pounds rabbit meat

1. Puncture and drain the coconut, setting aside the milk. Crack the coconut; remove the meat. Pare off the brown lining and cut the coconut meat into chunks.

2. Put the coconut meat, coconut milk, and water into a blender; blend until smooth. Heat to a boil in a large saucepan and simmer 15 minutes to thicken slightly. Transfer to the slow cooker.

3. Mince the tomatoes and onions. Add the tomatoes, onions, salt, and pepper to the coconut.

4. Cut the rabbit meat into serving-size pieces. Add to the coconut mixture. Cover and heat on a low setting for 4 to 6 hours, basting often.

Sweet Red Peppers

Does your dish call for sweet red peppers? If so, set some raw slices aside to add to your dishes as a crisp, tasty garnish. This will add color as well as flavor to whatever dish you have in the works.

Slow Venison

As with wild poultry, the secret to cooking wild game is to age the meat.
Do this by marinating it in your refrigerator for an extra-long time.

Serves 6–8

Cooking time: 4–6 hours
Preparation time: 30 minutes
Attention: Moderate
Pot size: 3–5 quarts

3 pounds venison roast
3 cups red wine
3 tablespoons olive oil
3 bay leaves
10 whole cloves

1. Slice the meat. Cover with wine and marinate in the refrigerator for 3 to 4 days. Strain and save 1 cup of marinade. Sauté the meat in oil in a pan over medium heat until browned. Transfer to the slow cooker with saved marinade and spices.

2. Cover and heat on low setting for 4 to 6 hours. Baste twice.

Fresh Is Not Always Best

Fresh wild game such as venison and rabbit should be aged in a cool, dry place for several days before cooking. Check with your local meat locker or other source of wild game to be sure they do this, or for guidance on how to do this yourself for different types of game.

chapter 11
europe and the mediterranean

Hungarian Sauerkraut

Serves 6–8

Cooking time: 4–6 hours
Preparation time: 30 minutes
Attention: Minimal
Pot size: 3–5 quarts

6 tomatoes
1 pound bacon
2 pounds sauerkraut
2 tablespoons paprika
1 tablespoon sugar
1 cup white wine
1 cup beef broth
1 bouquet garni

*This works well with Leo's Savory Ham (page 122), on a Classic Reuben
(page 96), or on a Sausage and Sauerkraut Sandwich (page 92).*

1. Chop the tomatoes; cut the bacon into 1-inch pieces. Drain the sauer-
    kraut. Divide the tomatoes, bacon, sauerkraut, and paprika each into
    two equal portions.

2. Make two layers in the slow cooker as follows: Bacon on the bottom, then
    sauerkraut, paprika, tomatoes; repeat. Sprinkle the top with the sugar.

3. Pour the wine and broth over the top. Add the bouquet garni.

4. Cover and heat on low setting for 4 to 6 hours.

German Carrot Soup

Garnish this soup with a sprinkle of fresh mint for an extra dash of color.
A food processor makes this dish easier.

1. Clean and grate the carrots; mince the onion.

2. Sauté the carrots and onion in butter in a pan over medium heat for 10 minutes. Add the carrot and onion mixture, broth, bouquet garni, cayenne pepper, salt, and egg noodles to the slow cooker.

3. Cover and heat on a high setting for 1 to 2 hours.

4. Half an hour before serving, turn the heat to low, remove the bouquet garni, and stir in the cream and egg yolks.

Serves 4–6

Cooking time: 1–2 hours
Preparation time: 30 minutes
Attention: Minimal
Pot size: 3–5 quarts

8 carrots
1 onion
2 tablespoons butter
2 cups chicken broth
1 bouquet garni
¼ teaspoon cayenne pepper
¼ teaspoon salt
¼ pound dried egg noodles
1 cup cream
2 egg yolks

Chicken Mulligatawny Soup

When serving this dish, also provide toasted strips of fresh coconut, white raisins, and Apricot Peach Chutney (page 198).

Serves 6–8

Cooking time: 4–6 hours
Preparation time: 45 minutes
Attention: Minimal
Pot size: 3–5 quarts

*1 pound boneless, skinless
   chicken breast*
3 tablespoons butter
2 apples
2 onions
¼ cup flour
1½ tablespoons curry powder
6 cups chicken broth
1 cup uncooked rice
½ teaspoon salt

1. Cube the chicken. Sauté in butter in a pan over medium heat until lightly browned.

2. Core and cube the apples and mince the onions. Add the apples and onions to the chicken in the pan over medium heat and stir until the onions are soft. Add the flour and curry powder and stir to blend in.

3. Put the sautéed mixture, broth, rice, and salt in the slow cooker.

4. Cover and heat on a low setting for 4 to 6 hours.

Dressing Up Curry
When serving curry, include a variety of garnishes from which guests can choose. Set out chutney, chopped peanuts or cashews, raisins stewed in brandy, sliced hard-boiled eggs, and grated coconut. Also provide thin banana and apple slices doused with lemon juice to prevent browning.

Spanish Beef Stew

For extra flavor, use wrinkled Turkish or other olives,
instead of the standard stuffed olives found in the grocery store.

Serves 4–6

Cooking time: 4–6 hours
Preparation time: 30 minutes
Attention: Minimal
Pot size: 3–5 quarts

1. Crush and slice the garlic; slice the onion. Cut the bacon into 1-inch lengths. Cube the beef. Sauté the garlic, onion, bacon, and beef in a pan over medium heat; drain and transfer the meat mixture to the slow cooker.

2. Dice the tomatoes. Crumble the bay leaf. Add the tomatoes, spices, salt, vinegar, stock, and wine to the slow cooker.

3. Cover and heat on a medium setting for 4 to 6 hours.

4. Dice the potatoes, slice the olives, and chop the parsley. An hour before serving, add the potatoes, olives, and parsley to the slow cooker.

2 cloves garlic
1 onion
3 slices bacon
1 pound beef
3 tomatoes
1 bay leaf
¼ teaspoon sage
¼ teaspoon marjoram
½ teaspoon paprika
½ teaspoon curry powder
1 teaspoon salt
2 tablespoons vinegar
1 cup stock
½ cup white wine
4 potatoes
⅓ cup olives
2 tablespoons parsley

Classic German Cabbage Rolls

Serve with black bread and garlic butter.
Save the broth from this recipe to use as a starter for some great soup.

Serves 6–8

Cooking time: 6–8 hours
Preparation time: 90 minutes
Attention: Minimal
Pot size: 3–5 quarts

1 head cabbage
1 onion
1 clove garlic
1 pound ground beef
1 pound ground sausage
¾ cup cooked rice
1½ teaspoons salt
½ teaspoon black pepper
1 cup water
2 cups vinegar

1. Boil one whole head of cabbage in a covered pot over high heat for 5 minutes. Cool; carefully separate the leaves and set aside.

2. Mince the onion and garlic. Mix with the meat, rice, salt, and pepper.

3. Put about ¼ cup of the meat mixture onto each cabbage leaf, roll, and tuck in the ends. Arrange in the slow cooker. To secure the mound, top it with an inverted glass plate or glass bowl as a weight.

4. Add the water and vinegar.

5. Cover and heat on a low setting for 6 to 8 hours.

Using Labels on Dishes
Label your slow cookers with their contents so guests don't have to lift the lids and wonder, "What's in here?" Place the label on the table or on the wall behind the slow cooker—the appliance will likely be too hot to hold a label.

Country French Sauerkraut

*This isn't as rich as the original recipe, which calls for goose fat,
not goose meat, but it's just as delectable.*

Serves 8–10

Cooking time: 5–6 hours
Preparation time: 30 minutes
Attention: Moderate
Pot size: 5 quarts

2 pounds bacon
½ pound goose meat
2 pounds sauerkraut
1 tablespoon whole
*   peppercorns*
2 cups white wine
2 cups beef bouillon

1. Sauté two slices of the bacon in a pan over medium heat until browned. Cut the goose meat into 1-inch cubes; sauté in the pan with the bacon over medium heat until the goose is lightly browned. Drain the meat. Set aside the two cooked bacon strips.

2. Cut the remaining, uncooked bacon into 1-inch lengths. Divide the browned goose meat into two equal portions; do the same for the sauerkraut and bacon.

3. Assemble layers in the slow cooker, in this order: Raw bacon (on the bottom), goose, sauerkraut, raw bacon, goose, sauerkraut. Sprinkle each layer with a few peppercorns.

4. Pour the wine and bouillon over the layers. Cover and heat on low setting for 5 to 6 hours.

5. Before serving, remove the excess liquid from the slow cooker, enough to expose the top of the layered ingredients. Sprinkle the sauerkraut with the set-aside bacon, crumbled.

Jacques' White Beans

Depending on your schedule, you can complete some parts of this recipe in advance, and save the final assembly until just before your party.

Serves 10–12

Cooking time: 7–9 hours
Preparation time: 45 minutes
Attention: Moderate
Pot size: 5 quarts

2 pounds white beans
2 cups water
1 ham bone
1 bouquet garni
1 teaspoon salt
3 onions
1 clove garlic
3 tablespoons butter
¼ cup parsley
1 cup tomato sauce
½ teaspoon black pepper

1. Soak the beans overnight in cold water, then drain.

3. Combine 2 cups fresh water, beans, ham bone, bouquet garni, and salt in the slow cooker.

4. Cover and heat on a low setting for 6 to 8 hours. Remove the bone and bouquet garni; drain.

5. Dice the onions; crush and slice the garlic. Sauté the onions and garlic in butter in a pan over medium heat until soft. Chop the parsley.

2. An hour before serving, add the onion, garlic, parsley, tomato sauce, and black pepper to the beans in the slow cooker.

Mixing Bowls
Using the right kind of bowl will make mixing easier. Instead of a light bowl with steep sides, use a heavy mixing bowl with sloping sides. The weight will hold it in place, and the sides will let you slide your spoon around easier, without keeping your elbow up in the air.

Spanish Saffron Rice

This fragrant dish goes well with grilled chicken or fish and looks very festive alongside shish kebabs. Use saffron threads instead of powder, if possible.

Serves 6–8

Cooking time: 4–6 hours
Preparation time: 45 minutes
Attention: Minimal
Pot size: 3–5 quarts

1 onion
4 stalks celery
2 tablespoons olive oil
3 tomatoes
1⅓ cups uncooked rice
4 cups water
2 teaspoons salt
¼ teaspoon cayenne pepper
1 green pepper
¼ pound Gruyère cheese
½ teaspoon saffron threads

1. Thinly slice the onion and celery. Sauté the onion and celery in oil in a pan over medium heat until soft. Transfer to the slow cooker.

2. Cube the tomatoes. Put the tomatoes, rice, water, salt, and cayenne pepper in the slow cooker.

3. Cover and heat on a low setting for 4 to 6 hours.

4. Mince the green pepper and grate the cheese. Half an hour before serving, stir in the green pepper, cheese, and saffron.

Serving Stations

Have you heard of multitasking? Try "multiserving" as well. Have slow cookers in three or four serving areas around your party zone, and guests will keep moving around to try all your creations. The more they move around, the more they will chat and enjoy each other.

Polish Bouja

You can use your food processor to speed up this recipe, if you wish.
Serve with pumpernickel rolls to soak up the juices.

Serves 4–6

Cooking time: 4–6 hours
Preparation time: 90 minutes
Attention: Minimal
Pot size: 5 quarts

1 pound chicken meat, boneless
4 potatoes
4 carrots
1 onion
1 pound fresh green beans
4 stalks celery
½ head cabbage
¾ cup water
¼ cup pearl barley
½ teaspoon salt
½ teaspoon peppercorns
1 teaspoon pickling spices, in
*   cloth bag*

1. Cube the chicken meat, potatoes, carrots, and onion. Cut the beans into ½-inch lengths. Thinly slice the celery. Shred the cabbage.

2. Add the cut ingredients, water, barley, salt, and peppercorns to the slow cooker.

3. Cover and heat on a low setting for 4 to 6 hours.

4. Half an hour before serving, add the bag of pickling spices. Remove the bag before serving.

Prussian Cabbage

Serve this hot with cold sliced beef and hard sourdough rolls.
Also, provide some scorching horseradish and English mustard on the side.

Serves 6

Cooking time: 2–3 hours
Preparation time: 15 minutes
Attention: Minimal
Pot size: 3–5 quarts

1 head red cabbage
3 apples
4 slices bacon
½ cup vinegar
2 cups beef broth
½ teaspoon salt

1. Finely slice the red cabbage. Core and slice the apples. Cut the bacon into 1-inch lengths.

2. Arrange the cabbage, apples, and bacon in the slow cooker.

3. Add the vinegar, beef broth, and salt.

4. Cover and heat on a high setting for 2 to 3 hours.

O'Riley's Lamb Stew

*Serve this hearty stew with warm hunks of sourdough bread
and herbed butter for dipping.*

Serves 8–10

Cooking time: 4–6 hours
Preparation time: 30 minutes
Attention: Moderate
Pot size: 3–5 quarts

4 pounds lamb
1 pound baby carrots
1 pound red spring potatoes
½ pound pearl onions
½ teaspoon salt
2 cups water
1 bouquet garni
1 bunch parsley
½ cup flour
1 cup water
*1 tablespoon Worcestershire
sauce*

1. Cube the lamb. Heat it in water in a covered pot over high heat and boil 10 minutes, then drain. Transfer the meat to the slow cooker.

2. Scrub the potatoes. Halve the carrots and potatoes. Remove the outer layer from the pearl onions.

3. Combine the meat and vegetables with salt, 2 cups water, and the bouquet garni in the slow cooker.

4. Cover and heat on a low setting for 4 to 6 hours.

5. Chop the parsley. Half an hour before serving, remove the bouquet garni. Blend the flour and remaining water and stir slowly into the stew. Stir in the parsley and Worcestershire sauce.

For the Carb Conscious

Cutting carbs? Play a trick on your taste buds. Replace ¼ cup of sugar in your recipe with a pinch of salt. It will bring out the natural sweetness of the other ingredients. At least, that's what your taste buds will think.

Hungarian Goulash

Serves 6–8

Cooking time: 4–6 hours
Preparation time: 45 minutes
Attention: Minimal
Pot size: 3–5 quarts

2 onions
3 tablespoons butter
1 pound beef
1 pound pork
2 tablespoons flour
½ teaspoon salt
½ teaspoon pepper
2 tablespoons paprika
¼ cup celery
3 potatoes
1 cup beef stock
1 cup tomato sauce
½ teaspoon salt
½ teaspoon thyme
1 bay leaf
2 whole cloves
¼ cup parsley

*This dish freezes well. Keep a batch set aside for unexpected company,
then reheat and add a fresh parsley garnish.*

1. Chop the onions and sauté in butter in a pan over medium heat until browned. Cube the meat and add to the onions. Sauté over medium heat until browned.

2. Mix the flour with ½ teaspoon salt, pepper, and paprika. Stir the flour mixture into the meat and onions. Transfer the meat mixture to the slow cooker.

3. Chop the celery into ½-inch lengths; cut the potatoes into 1-inch cubes. Add the celery, potatoes, stock, tomato sauce, ½ teaspoon salt, and spices to the slow cooker. Cover and heat on a low setting for 4 to 6 hours.

4. Chop the parsley. Before serving, remove the bay leaf and stir in the parsley.

Think Variety

When planning a menu, think about colors, smells, and textures of individual servings. How would these three dishes look next to each other? Are there some salty, crunchy foods as well as soft, delicate foods?

Aromatic Paella

This is a fun dish for a slow cooker.
The mussels and clams open during the cooking and flavor the rice.

Serves 10–12

Cooking time: 4–6 hours
Preparation time: 60 minutes
Attention: Minimal
Pot size: 5 quarts

1. Thinly slice the onions. Sauté with the sausage in oil in a pan over low heat until the sausage is crumbled and browned, then drain and transfer to the slow cooker.

2. Crush the garlic and dice the tomatoes; stir in with the sausage and onions. Add the liquids, rice, spices, and salt.

3. Cover and heat on a low setting for 4 to 6 hours.

4. Cube the fish. Sauté the fish and shrimp in the remaining oil. Clean the mollusk shells. Do not steam them.

5. Dice the green pepper. An hour before serving, add the seafood, green pepper, and peas to the slow cooker.

2 onions
1 pound bulk spicy sausage
1 tablespoon olive oil
4 cloves garlic
2 pounds tomatoes
16 ounces clam juice
2 cups chicken broth
1 cup dry vermouth
2½ cups uncooked rice
2 teaspoons coriander
½ teaspoon cumin
1 teaspoon saffron
¼ teaspoon white pepper
¼ teaspoon salt
1 pound fish
1 pound shrimp
2 tablespoons olive oil
1 pound fresh mussels
1 pound fresh clams
1 green pepper
1 cup fresh green peas

All about Aroma

Once they're opened, slow cookers full of food will release a strong aroma. Try putting different slow cookers in different areas of your entertaining space, even in separate rooms. Have a "dessert room," a "spicy room," and a "bakery" room and let your guests move freely between them.

German Breakfast Eggs

This dish is delicious on a crisp morning.
Serve these eggs with fried tomatoes and fresh coffee.

Serves 6

Cooking time: 3–4 hours
Preparation time: 30 minutes
Attention: Minimal
Pot size: 3–5 quarts

6 potatoes
2 tablespoons butter
4 eggs
2 cups light cream
1 teaspoon salt
2 tablespoons flour
½ cup light cream

1. Shred the potatoes.

2. Butter the inside of the slow cooker.

3. Beat the eggs; mix in 2 cups light cream, salt, and flour.

4. Pour the egg mixture into the slow cooker. Add the potatoes. Pour the remaining ½ cup of cream over the top.

5. Cover and heat on a low setting for 3 to 4 hours.

The Skinny on Creams

If you don't have any cream handy (either light or heavy) but want to use it for cooking, you can substitute. For 1 cup heavy cream, substitute ¾ cup milk and 1/3 cup melted butter. For 1 cup light cream, use 1 cup undiluted evaporated milk or ¾ cup milk and ¼ cup melted butter.

Chicken Budapest

This goes well with a side dish of steamed baby asparagus, baby carrots, and small red potatoes with cracked black peppercorns.

1. Mix the flour, salt, and pepper. Cut the chicken into serving-size pieces and coat with the flour mixture. Sauté the chicken pieces in oil in a pan over medium heat until the meat is lightly browned.

2. Slice the onions. Crush and slice the garlic. Add the onion and garlic to the pan with the chicken and stir over medium heat until the onion is soft. Add the paprika to the pan and stir to mix.

3. Add the chicken-and-onion mixture and 2 cups of water to the slow cooker.

4. Cover and heat on a low setting for 4 to 6 hours.

5. Mix the remaining water and flour in a mixing bowl, then add the sour cream and blend well. An hour before serving, slowly stir the sour cream mixture into the chicken.

Go Nuts!
If your recipe calls for walnuts, be bold and try macadamias, hazelnuts, cashews, or pecans. Go out of your way to find new nuts to use in your recipes. Start with raw, unsalted nuts if you can get them, otherwise eliminate or reduce the amount of salt you add to the recipe.

Serves 5–6

Cooking time: 4–6 hours
Preparation time: 45 minutes
Attention: Moderate
Pot size: 3–5 quarts

1 cup flour
½ teaspoon salt
½ teaspoon white pepper
2½ pounds chicken
3 tablespoons oil
2 onions
3 cloves garlic
3 tablespoons paprika
2 cups water
½ cup water
2 tablespoons flour
2 cups sour cream

Royal Stew

This classic recipe is a thrifty way to get the most use out of juicy soup bones.
Ask your butcher to crack them for you.

Serves 5–6

Cooking time: 4–6 hours
Preparation time: 45 minutes
Attention: Moderate
Pot size: 3–5 quarts

1 onion
1 leek
1 stalk celery
2 tablespoons olive oil
¼ pound butter
¼ cup flour
2 large carrots
1 cup green peas
5 pounds fresh beef bones
3 cups water
1 bouquet garni
½ cup sherry

1. Thinly slice the onion, leek, and celery and combine. Sauté the sliced onion mixture in oil in a pan over medium heat until soft. Transfer to the slow cooker.

2. Melt the butter in the same pan over medium heat. Add the flour to the melted butter and stir until the flour is lightly browned. Transfer to the slow cooker; stir into the onion mixture.

3. Slice the carrots. Add the carrots, peas, beef bones, water, and bouquet garni to the slow cooker.

4. Cover and heat on a low setting for 4 to 6 hours.

5. Half an hour before serving, remove the beef bones and bouquet garni, then add the sherry.

Be Patient—Don't Peek

Keeping the lid on is the whole trick to slow cooking. The steam has to build up inside the cooker, and it takes time (about 15 minutes) to do so. Each time you lift the lid, the steam escapes, adding another 15 minutes to cooking time.

Old Country Mulled Wine

*If possible, try this recipe with tangerines or tangelos instead of oranges.
These will give the dish an entirely different flavor.*

1. Peel the lemon and orange halves. Remove and discard the pulp and the white lining of the peels; cut the colored peel portions into thin strips and transfer to the slow cooker. Add the wine, sugar, and spices.

2. Cover and heat on a low setting for 2 to 3 hours.

3. Thinly slice the orange in cross sections. An hour before serving, add the orange slices to the slow cooker.

Surprise Party

You can turn take-out pizza with friends into a party. Bring out a bucket of vanilla ice cream for dessert, and unveil five steaming slow cookers full of hot sundae toppings. Try Brandy Sauce (page 44), Tangiers Orange Sauce (page 46), Got-to-Have-It Chocolate Sauce (page 47), Figs in Cognac (page 244), and Spiced Cherries (page 251).

Serves 4–6

Cooking time: 3–4 hours
Preparation time: 2 hours
Attention: Minimal
Pot size: 3–5 quarts

½ lemon
½ orange
1 bottle claret wine
¼ cup sugar
3-inch stick cinnamon bark
¼ teaspoon ground nutmeg
6 whole cloves
1 orange

St. Regal Wine Sauce

*Choose a nice dry wine for this recipe, or experiment with
a sherry or brandy of your choice. This is delicious over chicken breast.*

Yields 20

Cooking time: 3–5 hours
Preparation time: 30 minutes
Attention: Moderate
Pot size: 3–5 quarts

1 lemon
2 cups water
1 cup sugar
1 teaspoon cornstarch
2 tablespoons water
1 cup wine

1. Grate half of the lemon rind; set aside. Cut the lemon in half and press to extract the juice of the entire lemon; save the juice and discard the lemon pulp.

2. Add the grated rind (from half the lemon), juice (from the whole lemon), water, and sugar to the slow cooker.

3. Cover and heat on a low setting for 1 to 2 hours.

4. Dissolve the cornstarch in 2 tablespoons cold water. Add to the sugar mixture in the slow cooker.

5. Cover and heat on a low setting for 1 to 2 hours.

6. An hour before serving, add the wine.

chapter 12
the far east

Greek Dolmades

Grape leaves are often sold pickled in jars.
If you can't get them at your local market, you can substitute cabbage leaves.

Yields about 20 rolls

Cooking time: 3–4 hours
Preparation time: 2 hours
Attention: Moderate
Pot size: 3–5 quarts

½ pound ground beef
½ pound ground lamb
1 egg
1 onion
1 bunch parsley
4–6 fresh mint leaves
½ cup uncooked rice
2 tablespoons olive oil
¼ cup water
¼ teaspoon salt
¼ teaspoon black pepper
20 grape leaves
1½ cups beef broth
1½ cups water
2 eggs
Juice of 1 lemon

1. Mix the beef, lamb, and egg. Mince the onion; chop the parsley and mint leaves. Add the onion, parsley, mint, rice, olive oil, water, salt, and pepper to the meat mixture.

2. Put 1 to 2 teaspoons of the meat mixture on each grape leaf, shiny side down, sealing the ends inside. Arrange the folded side down on a rack in the slow cooker. Place a glass plate or bowl on top to weight down the mound.

3. Pour the broth and water over the rolls.

4. Cover and heat on a high setting for 3 to 4 hours.

5. Before serving, beat the eggs in a large mixing bowl and stir the lemon juice into the eggs. Slowly add ½ cup of the hot broth from the slow cooker to the egg mixture and continue mixing. Drain most of the broth from the rolls and add it to the egg mixture. Provide this separately as a sauce.

Get Help and Get Relaxed
Even if you can't afford professionals to run your party, think about hiring or borrowing some helpers. Hire a local college student home on break to garnish your dishes and decorate your house. She'll appreciate the extra money and you'll appreciate the help.

Japanese Custard

This delicate custardlike soup goes well with grilled fish and vegetables, or as part of a light meal with a green salad.

1. Beat the eggs well. Mix with the chicken broth and salt in a mixing bowl.

2. Dice the mushrooms, chicken, and green onions; sauté in rice oil in a pan over low heat until the mushrooms are soft.

3. Distribute the mushroom mixture and rice between 4 custard cups. Divide the broth mixture between the same custard cups; top each with a lid of glass.

4. Arrange the dishes on a trivet in the slow cooker. Pour water around the base.

5. Cover and heat on a high setting for 1 to 2 hours.

Try Something New
Perhaps you've noticed an ethnic grocery store down the street or near your office. Go in and take a look. Even if you can't read the labels, there might be a picture, or you could be brave and try something you can't identify. This is an excellent way to find new ingredients unavailable in standard grocery stores, like wide varieties of olives, flatbreads, chili powders, curries, coconut milk, exotic fruits, and much more.

Serves 4

Cooking time: 1–2 hours
Preparation time: 45 minutes
Attention: Minimal
Pot size: 3–5 quarts

2 eggs
2 cups chicken broth
¼ teaspoon salt
¼ pound mushrooms
¼ pound boneless, skinless chicken
4 green onions
1 teaspoon rice oil
¼ cup cooked rice

Gingery Pumpkin Soup

*You can use raw butternut or acorn squash instead of pumpkin,
or add some brown sugar or maple syrup for an extra hint of autumn.*

Serves 6

Cooking time: 5–6 hours
Preparation time: 30 minutes
Attention: Moderate
Pot size: 3–5 quarts

2 pounds raw pumpkin
1 onion
2 cloves
3 cups chicken stock
¼ teaspoon cinnamon
2 tablespoons fresh ginger
½ teaspoon black pepper
¼ teaspoon salt
1 cup heavy cream

1. Peel the pumpkin; remove the seeds and cube the flesh. Peel the onion and stick the cloves in the whole, peeled onion.

2. Transfer the pumpkin, onion, stock, spices, and salt to the slow cooker.

3. Cover and heat on a low setting for 4 to 5 hours.

4. An hour before serving, remove the onion. Lift out some of the pumpkin chunks and puree with the cream in a blender or food processor. Add the creamed mixture to the slow cooker.

Katie's Chai

*Chai is stewed to caramelize the milk sugars, which completely changes the
taste. In Asian countries street vendors sell it by cupfuls from steaming kettles.*

Serves 6

Cooking time: 3–4 hours
Preparation time: 30 minutes
Attention: Moderate
Pot size: 3–5 quarts

3 cups milk
3 cups water
½ cup loose tea leaves
¾ cup sugar
3 cardamom pods
4 whole cloves
¼ vanilla bean pod

1. Combine the ingredients in the slow cooker. Stir to be sure the sugar is dissolved.

2. Cover and heat on a low setting for 3 to 4 hours.

3. Remove the pods and skim the surface to remove any floating tea leaves before serving.

Ginger Tomato Lamb

You can substitute beef or pork for lamb in this recipe if you wish.
Serve with triangles of fresh pita bread.

Serves 4–6

Cooking time: 4–5 hours
Preparation time: 30 minutes
Attention: Minimal
Pot size: 3–5 quarts

2 pounds lamb
2 tablespoons butter
1 onion
1 clove garlic
3 tablespoons flour
1½ tablespoons curry powder
2 tomatoes
1 inch fresh gingerroot
1 teaspoon salt
¼ cup water

1. Cube the lamb. Sauté in butter in a pan over medium heat until slightly browned. Transfer the meat to the slow cooker; set aside the pan with the juices.

2. Chop the onion; crush and mince the garlic. Add the onion and garlic to the pan used for the lamb and sauté over medium heat until the onion is tender. Stir in the flour and curry and mix while heating. When thickened, add the onion mixture to the slow cooker.

3. Chop the tomatoes. Peel and grate the gingerroot. Add the tomatoes, ginger, salt, and water to the slow cooker.

4. Cover and heat on a low setting for 4 to 5 hours.

Custom Curry Sauce

Cooking time: 3–4 hours
Preparation time: 60 minutes
Attention: Minimal
Pot size: 3–5 quarts

1 onion
1 leek
1 clove garlic
2 stalks celery
1 bay leaf
1 teaspoon thyme
4 tablespoons butter
2 tablespoons curry powder
2 tablespoons flour
2 cups meat or seafood stock
¼ teaspoon salt
1 banana
1 apple
½ cup chutney

Use this sauce with any kind of meat or seafood you like.
Just use the stock that corresponds with the meat you choose.

1. Thinly slice the onion, leek, garlic, and celery; combine. Sauté the sliced mixture, bay leaf, and thyme in 3 tablespoons of the butter in a pan over medium heat until the onion is soft. Add the curry powder and flour; stir while heating for 5 minutes.

2. Add the curry mixture, stock, and salt to the slow cooker.

3. Cover and heat on low setting for 2 to 3 hours.

4. Slice the banana and sauté in 1 tablespoon butter in a pan over medium heat until browned. Peel, core, and mince the apple.

5. An hour before serving, add the banana, apple, and chutney to the slow cooker.

Almond Chicken Gifts

Grated fresh gingerroot and mandarin orange segments are excellent condiments for these treats. Serve with white or stir-fried rice.

1. Mince the chicken and almonds. Beat the eggs and stir in the chicken, almonds, and soy sauce.

2. Clean the spinach leaves. Place a teaspoon of the chicken mixture on each leaf. Fold the leaves over the chicken mixture, forming a roll, and tie with cotton string.

3. Arrange the rolls on a rack in the slow cooker. Pour the wine and water around the base.

4. Cover and cook on a high setting for 2 to 3 hours.

Serves 6–8

Cooking time: 2–3 hours
Preparation time: 30 minutes
Attention: Minimal
Pot size: 3–5 quarts

1 pound boneless, skinless chicken
½ cup almonds
2 eggs
2 tablespoons soy sauce
30–35 large spinach leaves
½ cup white wine
1 cup water

Tropical Bread Pudding

*If you can't get fresh or canned coconut milk for this recipe,
you can make your own Coconut Milk (page 193).*

Yields about 2 loaves

Cooking time: 3–4 hours
Preparation time: 30 minutes
Attention: Minimal
Pot size: 3–5 quarts

6 eggs
½ cup brown sugar
1 teaspoon cinnamon
2 cups coconut milk
10 slices stale bread
*½ pound pineapple, peeled
    and cored*
2 tablespoons butter
Rind of ½ lemon

1. Beat the eggs. Add the sugar, cinnamon, and coconut milk; mix well.

2. Cube the bread. Dice the pineapple. Butter 2 loaf pans or the equivalent. Arrange the bread and pineapple in the baking dishes.

3. Grate the lemon rind. Sprinkle the grated rind and pour the milk mixture over the bread, filling the dishes no more than ½ full.

4. Loosely cover each dish with a foil or glass lid. Place on a trivet or rack in the slow cooker, and pour water around the base of the trivet.

5. Cover and heat on a high setting for 2 to 3 hours.

Ghee

Store this in glass jars in the refrigerator.
If the recipe you're using it in calls for liquid ghee, warm the ghee before using.

Yields about 3 cups

Cooking time: 2–3 hours
Preparation time: 15 minutes
Attention: Moderate
Pot size: 3–5 quarts

2 pounds butter, unsalted

1. Cut the butter into large cubes.

2. Cover and heat on a low setting for 2 to 3 hours. The butter should separate. Don't let it brown.

3. Skim off the clear liquid on the top; this is ghee. Store refrigerated and covered. Discard the butter solids, or use in cooking as a butter substitute.

Coconut Milk

The milk and "used" coconut solids can be frozen for later use
in curries, sauces, puddings, and cakes.

Yields about 3 cups

Cooking time: 2–3 hours
Preparation time: 30 minutes
Attention: Minimal
Pot size: 3–5 quarts

2 cups coconut pieces
2 cups water

1. Remove any remaining coconut shell or brown lining from the coconut meat. Put the coconut meat and water in the blender. Blend until smooth.

2. Transfer to the slow cooker.

3. Cover and heat on a low setting for 2 to 3 hours. Strain.

Indian Lentils

Look for orange lentils in your local market or an international grocery.
Brown lentils give an entirely different taste and texture.

Serves 6

Cooking time: 3–4 hours
Preparation time: 30 minutes
Attention: Minimal
Pot size: 3–5 quarts

1 onion
3 cloves garlic
1 green pepper
1 teaspoon cumin
2 tablespoons Ghee (page 193)
2 cups cubed tomatoes
1½ cups orange lentils
3 cups water
2 teaspoons honey
¼ teaspoon salt

1. Slice the onion and garlic; dice the green pepper. Sauté the onion, garlic, and green pepper with cumin in Ghee in a pan over medium heat until the onion is soft.

2. Add the tomatoes, onion mixture, lentils, water, honey, and salt to the slow cooker.

3. Cover and heat on a low setting for 3 to 4 hours.

Coconut Rice

Try adding white raisins or small pieces of fresh pineapple
to this dish during the last hour of cooking.

Serves 4–6

Cooking time: 4–5 hours
Preparation time: 15 minutes
Attention: Minimal
Pot size: 3–5 quarts

1 lemon
1 cup uncooked rice
2 cups coconut milk
½ cup water
½ teaspoon salt
½ teaspoon turmeric
¼ cup toasted pistachios

1. Squeeze the juice from the lemon. Put the lemon juice, rice, coconut milk, water, salt, and turmeric in the slow cooker.

2. Cover and heat on a low setting for 3 to 4 hours.

3. Chop the pistachios into coarse pieces. An hour before serving, stir in the pistachios.

Eastern Lamb Curry

This should be served with rice, preferably basmati rice.
Provide condiments, including white raisins, toasted coconut shavings,
and roasted cashews or pistachios.

Serves 6–8

Cooking time: 3–4 hours
Preparation time: 60 minutes
Attention: Minimal
Pot size: 3–5 quarts

3 pounds lamb
1 carrot
1 onion
3 cups water
1 bouquet garni
½ teaspoon salt
1 banana
5 tablespoons butter
2 tablespoons curry powder
2 tablespoons flour
1 apple
½ cup chutney

1. Cube the lamb. Clean and peel the carrot and onion. Put the meat in a stockpot with the carrot, onion, water, bouquet garni, and salt; boil for 20 minutes.

2. After boiling, remove and discard the carrot, onion, and bouquet garni. Skim the surface of the boiled water and discard any debris. Transfer the meat and liquid to the slow cooker.

3. Slice the banana in ½-inch slices. Sauté in 2 tablespoons of the butter in a pan over low heat until the banana is lightly browned. Transfer the banana and juices to the slow cooker.

4. In the same pan, melt the remaining butter. Add the curry and flour, then stir over low heat for 5 minutes. Core and cube the apple; stir the apple and chutney into the curry mixture. Transfer the curry mixture to the slow cooker.

5. Cover and heat on a low setting for 3 to 4 hours.

Alcohol Alert

Always keep some foods and drinks alcohol-free. As a courtesy, label all dishes so guests don't have to ask if something contains alcohol. This way, they won't make an unfortunate assumption.

Mountain Honey Lamb with Dates

You can buy ghee for this recipe, or make your own Ghee (page 193).
Serve this with warm, fresh pita bread.

Serves 6–8

Cooking time: 5–6 hours
Preparation time: 30 minutes
Attention: Minimal
Pot size: 3–5 quarts

2 pounds lamb
1 onion
5 tablespoons Ghee (page 193)
1 cup dates
1 teaspoon turmeric
1 teaspoon cinnamon
½ teaspoon salt
2 tablespoons honey
1 cup uncooked rice
2½ cups water
Rind of ¼ lemon

1. Cut the lamb into cubes; slice the onion. Sauté the lamb and onion in 3 tablespoons of the Ghee in a pan over medium heat until the meat is lightly browned.

2. Pit and chop the dates. Add the meat mixture, dates, spices, salt, honey, rice, and water to the slow cooker.

3. Cover and heat on a low setting for 4 to 5 hours.

4. Finely grate the lemon rind. Half an hour before serving, add the lemon rind and the remaining Ghee.

Simple Curry Chicken

This basic curry can be served with rice, preferably basmati.
Dress it up with a variety of condiments if your schedule allows.

Serves 6–8

Cooking time: 2–3 hours
Preparation time: 15 minutes
Attention: Minimal
Pot size: 3–5 quarts

2 onions
3 pounds chicken breasts
¼ cup olive oil
⅓ cup curry powder
½ cup water

1. Dice the onions and cut the chicken into serving-size pieces. Sauté the onions in oil in a pan over medium heat until browned. Slowly stir in the curry powder, then add the chicken breasts and sauté over medium heat until lightly browned.

2. Put the chicken mixture and water in the slow cooker.

3. Cover and heat on a low setting for 2 to 3 hours.

Soy and Chestnut Chicken

Garnish this with roasted soy nuts and mung bean sprouts.
It's also very good chilled and sliced over salad greens.

1. Cut the chicken into serving-size pieces. Thinly slice the water chestnuts and cube the green pepper. Put the chicken, cut vegetables, soy sauce, and vinegar in the slow cooker.

2. Cover and heat on a low setting for 2 to 3 hours.

Serves 6–8

Cooking time: 2–3 hours
Preparation time: 15 minutes
Attention: Minimal
Pot size: 3–5 quarts

3 pounds chicken
1 pound canned water chestnuts
1 green bell pepper
1 cup soy sauce
½ cup vinegar

Nomad's Fruit and Nut Dish

This flavorful dish, made from ingredients that store well, is served over rice.
This is also excellent served with lamb chops.

1. Use kitchen shears to finely mince the orange rind. Chop the nuts and fruits. Diagonally slice the carrots.

2. Combine the rind, nuts, fruits, carrots, sugar, and water in the slow cooker.

3. Cover and heat on a low setting for 4 to 5 hours.

Serves 4–6

Cooking time: 4–5 hours
Preparation time: 15 minutes
Attention: Minimal
Pot size: 3–5 quarts

1 tablespoon dried orange rind
¼ cup shaved blanched almonds
¼ cup toasted pistachio nuts
¼ cup raisins
¼ cup dried apricots
4 carrots
¼ cup sugar
2 cups water

Ginger Barbecue Beef

Fresh ginger has a much more potent flavor than powdered, dried ginger.
Try to use the fresh root if available.

Serves 6–8

Cooking time: 4–5 hours
Preparation time: 30 minutes
Attention: Minimal
Pot size: 3–5 quarts

3 cloves garlic
1 inch fresh gingerroot
½ cup soy sauce
½ cup water
2 tablespoons sesame oil
2 tablespoons sugar
4 teaspoons sesame seeds
3 pounds beef
1 onion

1. Peel and mince the garlic and ginger. Mix in a small bowl with the soy sauce, water, oil, sugar, and sesame seeds.

2. Cut the beef in slices. Coarsely chop the onion.

3. Arrange the beef and onion in the slow cooker while sprinkling it throughout with the sauce mixture.

4. Cover and heat on a low setting for 4 to 5 hours.

Apricot Peach Chutney

This is excellent over hot sliced pork on rye toast.
Use this chutney as a condiment for curries and meats, too.

Yields about 2½ cups

Cooking time: 2–3 hours
Preparation time: 30 minutes
Attention: Minimal
Pot size: 3–5 quarts

1 onion
1 tablespoon oil
½ cup dried apricots
½ cup raisins
1 cup peach marmalade
½ cup white vinegar
½ cup brown sugar
1 tablespoon mustard seeds
½ cup water

1. Thinly slice the onion; sauté in oil in a pan over low heat until soft.

2. Cut the apricots into strips.

3. Combine the onion, apricots, raisins, marmalade, vinegar, sugar, mustard seeds, and water in the slow cooker.

4. Cover and heat on a low setting for 2 to 3 hours.

chapter 13
recipes from latin america

Mountain Garden Stew

*This is a good dish to provide for the vegetarians in your crowd,
or to serve with a grilled steak.*

Cooking time: 4–5 hours
Preparation time: 30 minutes
Attention: Minimal
Pot size: 3–5 quarts

3 onions
3 cloves garlic
2 tablespoons olive oil
1 pound squash
2 cups chopped tomatoes
1 teaspoon basil
1 teaspoon oregano
4 cups cooked navy beans
1 cup corn kernels
½ teaspoon salt
¼ teaspoon black pepper

1. Chop the onions and mince the garlic. Sauté the onions and garlic in oil in a pan over medium heat until soft.

2. Chop the squash and remove the squash seeds. Add the tomatoes, squash, and herbs to the slow cooker.

3. Cover and heat on a low setting for 3 to 4 hours.

4. An hour before serving, add the beans, corn, salt, and pepper to the slow cooker.

Curry and Zucchini Soup

*If you or a neighbor has zucchini in the garden, use it in this soup.
Fresh garden vegetables always provide great flavor.*

1. Coarsely chop the zucchini and onions.

2. Combine the zucchini, onions, broth, and curry powder in the slow cooker.

3. Cover and heat on a low setting for 2 to 3 hours.

4. Half an hour before serving, transfer some of the zucchini and onions with a slotted spoon to a blender or food processor and puree with the cream, salt, and pepper; return the pureed material to the slow cooker.

Serves 6–8

Cooking time: 3–4 hours
Preparation time: 30 minutes
Attention: Moderate
Pot size: 3–5 quarts

3 zucchini
2 onions
4 cups chicken broth
1 tablespoon curry powder
1 cup cream
½ teaspoon salt
½ teaspoon pepper

Equatorial Bread Pudding

This bread pudding has fruits, nuts, and cheese instead of eggs and milk as in the traditional continental U.S. version.

Serves 4–6

Cooking time: 2–3 hours
Preparation time: 15 minutes
Attention: Minimal
Pot size: 3–5 quarts

8 slices white bread
2 apples
½ pound cheese of choice
2 tablespoons butter
½ cup raisins
½ cup shelled peanuts
2 cups brown sugar
3 cups water
2 teaspoons cinnamon
½ teaspoon cloves

1. Remove the crusts from the bread; cube and toast it. Peel, core, and finely slice the apples. Shred the cheese.

2. Butter the inside of the slow cooker. Place half of the bread cubes in the bottom of the slow cooker. Then add the apples, raisins, and peanuts. Cover with the rest of the bread cubes, and put the cheese on top.

3. Combine the brown sugar, water, and spices. Pour this syrup over the whole mixture.

4. Cover and heat on a low setting for 2 to 3 hours.

Colombian Beef Stew

You can substitute pork for beef in this recipe, if you wish.
Use ears of fresh sweet corn, if possible.

Serves 6–8

Cooking time: 3–4 hours
Preparation time: 45 minutes
Attention: Minimal
Pot size: 3–5 quarts

1 onion
3 cloves garlic
2 tablespoons oil
2 pounds beef
3 potatoes
4 carrots
1 cup chopped tomatoes
3 cups water
1 teaspoon cumin
4 ears corn
1 cup green peas
½ teaspoon salt
¼ teaspoon pepper

1. Coarsely chop the onion and finely chop the garlic. Heat the onion and garlic in oil in a pan over medium heat until soft.

2. Cube the beef. Add the beef to the onion mixture and continue stirring over medium heat until the beef is browned.

3. Chop the potatoes; slice the carrots. Put the beef mixture, chopped tomatoes, and cut vegetables in the slow cooker with the water and cumin.

4. Cover and heat on a low setting for 3 to 4 hours.

5. Cut the corn ears into 1-inch lengths. An hour before serving, add the corn, peas, salt, and pepper.

Cooking Gloves
To avoid accidental burns from spattering, keep a pair of clean canvas gardening gloves in the kitchen to wear while stirring hot soups, sautéing meats or vegetables, or putting pasta into boiling water.

Brazilian Meat Stew

This goes well with fluffy white rice and a nice after-dinner coffee.
You can substitute salt pork for the bacon.

Serves 8–10

Cooking time: 3–4 hours
Preparation time: 30 minutes
Attention: Minimal
Pot size: 3–5 quarts

3 slices bacon
2 onions
3 cloves garlic
1 pound beef
1 pound pork
1 pound spicy link sausage
4 cups cooked black beans
    with liquid
2 cups chopped tomatoes
1 cup water
1 tablespoon prepared
    mustard
½ teaspoon salt
½ teaspoon pepper

1. Dice and sauté the bacon in a pan over medium heat until crispy.

2. Finely chop the onions and garlic. Add the onions and garlic to the bacon and continue heating until the onions are soft.

3. Cut the beef, pork, and sausage into bite-size pieces. Add the meat to the onion mixture and continue heating until the meat is browned. Transfer the meat-and-onion mixture to the slow cooker.

4. Mash 1 cup of the black beans and add both mashed and whole beans to the slow cooker. Add the tomatoes and the remaining ingredients to the slow cooker.

5. Cover and heat on a low setting for 3 to 4 hours.

Party Ice

If you're providing ice, make it party ice. Fill trays and pans with clean cookie cutters, then enough liquid to nearly cover the shapes. You can buy cookie cutters in the toy department or in craft stores. Use the fancy ice to hold bowls of dips or butter, or freeze shapes of fruit juice instead of water for flavored ice to put in punch.

Spices-of-Life Beef Stew

*This is your chance to take advantage of your spice collection.
However, if you have fresh parsley, use it instead of dried.*

Serves 6–8

Cooking time: 4–5 hours
Preparation time: 30 minutes
Attention: Minimal
Pot size: 3–5 quarts

1 pound beef
3 slices bacon
2 cloves garlic
1 onion
1 bay leaf
3 tomatoes
4 potatoes
¼ teaspoon sage
¼ teaspoon marjoram
½ teaspoon paprika
½ teaspoon curry powder
2 tablespoons vinegar
¾ cup stock
1 teaspoon salt
⅓ cup black olives
1 small bunch parsley
⅓ cup white wine

1. Cube the beef and dice the bacon. Crush the garlic and slice the onion. Sauté the beef, bacon, garlic, and onion in a pan over medium heat until the meat is browned. Transfer to the slow cooker.

2. Crumble the bay leaf. Dice the tomatoes and quarter the potatoes. Add the spices, tomatoes, potatoes, vinegar, stock, and salt to the slow cooker. Mix well.

3. Cover and heat on low setting for 3 to 4 hours.

4. Slice the olives and chop the parsley. Half an hour before serving, add the olives, parsley, and wine to the slow cooker.

Cutting Parsley

Need to chop a bunch of parsley? Don't use a knife. Instead, dip your clean pair of kitchen scissors in boiling water, hold your cleaned parsley over your mixing bowl or serving dishes, and snip away.

Mexico City Chocolate

You can add extra chocolate, or serve chocolates on the side with this hot drink. Keep the chocolates in a bowl sitting on ice.

Serves 4–6

Cooking time: 2–3 hours
Preparation time: 15 minutes
Attention: Moderate
Pot size: 3–5 quarts

4 cups milk
2 tablespoons strong coffee
½ cup water
2 squares sweetened
    chocolate
½ teaspoon nutmeg
1 1-inch stick cinnamon bark
½ teaspoon vanilla
⅛ teaspoon salt

1. Combine all ingredients, except vanilla and salt, in the slow cooker.

2. Cover and heat on a low setting for 2 to 3 hours.

3. Half an hour before serving, remove the cinnamon stick. Add the vanilla and salt and beat the mixture with an egg beater until foamy.

Creamy Corn Soup

This is a rich, delicious soup that is best served with hunks of crusty bread for dipping.

Serves 6–8

Cooking time: 4–5 hours
Preparation time: 30 minutes
Attention: Minimal
Pot size: 3–5 quarts

2 cloves garlic
1 pound tomatoes
3 cups chicken broth
2 cups corn kernels
1 teaspoon oregano
½ teaspoon salt
½ teaspoon black pepper
1 cup heavy cream
½ pound Romano cheese

1. Mince the garlic and chop the tomatoes.

2. Combine the ingredients, except cream and cheese, in slow cooker.

3. Cover and heat on low setting for 3 to 4 hours.

4. Half an hour before serving, stir in the cream.

5. Grate the cheese and provide as a garnish for individual servings.

Coconut Soup

This dish is simple but smooth and creamy.
You can also add rice, chicken, or seafood for other flavors and textures.

1. Finely chop the onion. Sauté in butter in a pan over medium heat until soft.

2. Blend the flour into ½ cup of the chicken broth. Add to the onion mixture and stir over medium heat until thickened.

3. Transfer to the slow cooker and add the remaining broth to the onion mixture.

4. Cover and heat on a low setting for 2 to 3 hours.

5. An hour before serving, add the coconut milk to the slow cooker.

Serves 6–8

Cooking time: 3–4 hours
Preparation time: 30 minutes
Attention: Minimal
Pot size: 3–5 quarts

1 onion
2 tablespoons butter
3 tablespoons flour
5 cups chicken broth
1¼ cups coconut milk

Banana Ribs

Bananas add a subtle sweetness to the meat.
If available, try tiny red bananas instead of the standard yellow.

Serves 10–12

Cooking time: 6–8 hours
Preparation time: 30 minutes
Attention: Minimal
Pot size: 3–5 quarts

4 potatoes
2 ears corn
1 bunch cilantro
1 teaspoon dried oregano
½ teaspoon salt
½ teaspoon black pepper
2 pounds beef ribs
2 onions
2 tomatoes
1 green bell pepper
3 bananas
4 cups beef broth

1. Peel the potatoes and cut them into 2-inch cubes. Husk and quarter the ears of corn. Put the potatoes and corn in the bottom of the slow cooker.

2. Chop the cilantro. Mix it in a small bowl with the oregano, salt, and black pepper. Sprinkle the vegetables in the slow cooker with one-third of the cilantro mixture.

3. Cut the ribs into serving-size pieces. Arrange in the slow cooker over the potatoes and corn. Sprinkle with one-third of the cilantro mixture.

4. Chop the onions, tomatoes, and green pepper. Peel the bananas and cut them into ½-inch slices. Arrange the cut vegetables and fruit over the meat in the slow cooker. Sprinkle with the remaining cilantro mixture.

5. Add the broth.

6. Cover and heat on a low setting for 6 to 8 hours.

Fresh Herbs or Dried?
Most recipes assume dried herbs will be used. However, if you happen to have fresh herbs, use them. For each teaspoon of herbs a recipe calls for, you can substitute a tablespoon of fresh ones.

Rancho Beef Casserole

In this recipe, corn tortillas are used to thicken the casserole.
Try this in other recipes to add a nice hint of corn flavor.

1. Finely chop the onion and garlic. Chop the green peppers; cube the beef.

2. Sauté the onion, garlic, peppers, beef, and chili powder in oil in a pan over medium heat until the meat is browned. Transfer the meat mixture to the slow cooker.

3. Chop the tomatoes. Add the tomatoes, water, spices, salt, and pepper to the slow cooker.

4. Cover and heat on a low setting for 3 to 4 hours.

5. Half an hour before serving, crumble the tortillas and add to the slow cooker to thicken. Remove bay leaves before serving.

Keep the Green

Tired of green peppers fading to a dull color during cooking? To preserve color when making stuffed green peppers, brush the outside of the pepper with oil before cooking. This is also why tossing them in the sauté pan briefly will help the color stay longer in other dishes.

Serves 6–8

Cooking time: 4–5 hours
Preparation time: 45 minutes
Attention: Minimal
Pot size: 3–5 quarts

1 onion
3 cloves garlic
2 green peppers
2 pounds beef
1 teaspoon chili powder
2 tablespoons oil
1 pound tomatoes
2 cups water
2 bay leaves
1 teaspoon ground cloves
1 teaspoon oregano
½ teaspoon salt
½ teaspoon pepper
2 corn tortillas

Light Tortilla Soup

Serves 6–8

Cooking time: 3–4 hours
Preparation time: 30 minutes
Attention: Minimal
Pot size: 3–5 quarts

½ onion
4 cups chicken broth
6 tablespoons tomato paste
½ teaspoon salt
¼ teaspoon white pepper
1 bunch cilantro
½ pound white cheese of
    choice
2 tortillas
¼ cup oil

*Here, tortillas are used not as a thickener, but as a crackly garnish.
Set out extras with salsa for your guests to snack on.*

1. Finely chop the onion. Combine the onion, broth, tomato paste, salt, and pepper in the slow cooker.

2. Cover and heat on a low setting for 2 to 3 hours.

3. Finely chop the cilantro. Half an hour before serving, add the cilantro to the slow cooker.

4. Shred the cheese. Slice the tortillas into strips and heat in oil in a pan over medium heat until browned. Transfer the tortilla strips to absorbent paper to drain. Provide the shredded cheese and tortilla strips as a garnish for individual servings.

Starch and Acid

More starch is needed to create the same thickness of a soup or sauce if an acid—like vinegar—is included. Extended cooking with acid present should be avoided when possible, or compensated for, because the acid will thin the starch.

Spiced Okra

This goes well with rice and grilled chicken.
Try using a bit of fresh gingerroot instead of ground ginger.

1. Mince the onion. Sauté the onion in butter in a pan over medium heat until soft.

2. Slice the okra. Add the okra, onion, water, and spices, and salt to the slow cooker.

3. Cover and heat on a low setting for 2 to 3 hours.

Serves 4–6

Cooking time: 2–3 hours
Preparation time: 30 minutes
Attention: Minimal
Pot size: 3–5 quarts

1 onion
3 tablespoons butter
2 pounds fresh okra
½ cup water
½ teaspoon cumin
½ teaspoon ginger
½ teaspoon coriander
¼ teaspoon black pepper
½ teaspoon salt

Cafe Vallarta

Use a potato peeler to shave thin orange peel twists from a fresh orange.
Avoid crushing the shavings, which releases their oils too early.

1. Combine the coffee, liqueurs, and sugar in the slow cooker.

2. Cover and heat on a low setting for 2 to 3 hours.

3. Provide the cinnamon and orange peels as garnish for individual servings.

Serves 6–8

Cooking time: 2–3 hours
Preparation time: 15 minutes
Attention: Minimal
Pot size: 3–5 quarts

8 cups coffee
8 ounces orange liqueur
8 ounces coffee liqueur
½ cup sugar
8 sticks cinnamon bark
8 orange peel twists

Peeling Oranges
To make peeling oranges easier, pour boiling water over the oranges and let them sit for five minutes. The white part will come off with the peel. Don't do this when the peel is needed for your recipe; it strips away some of the flavor.

Everything Stew

This unusual dish blends sweet flavors, including peaches, with vegetables and meat. Serve with a simple green salad with oil and vinegar.

Serves 12–14

Cooking time: 4–5 hours
Preparation time: 45 minutes
Attention: Minimal
Pot size: 3–5 quarts

2 onions
1 green pepper
2 tablespoons oil
2 pounds beef
1 pound tomatoes
1½ pounds sweet potatoes
1 pound squash
1 pound potatoes
2 cups corn kernels
2 cups water
4 peaches
½ teaspoon salt
¼ teaspoon pepper
2 tablespoons brown sugar

1. Finely chop the onions and green pepper. Sauté the onions and green pepper in oil in a pan over medium heat until soft.

2. Cube the meat. Add to the onion mixture and stir over medium heat until the meat is browned.

3. Cube the tomatoes, sweet potatoes, and squash; slice the potatoes. Add the cut vegetables, corn, and water to the slow cooker.

4. Cover and heat on a low setting for 3 to 4 hours.

5. Pit and slice the peaches. Half an hour before serving, add the peaches, salt, pepper, and sugar to the slow cooker.

Bug Sightings

Have you ever had the unfortunate experience of finding a small bug in your salad or steamed carrots? Don't despair. The solution is to add a little vinegar to the water you use when washing vegetables. This will rid your vegetables of insects in an instant.

chapter 14
beverages

Hot Mulled Cider

This classic is a must for the fall and winter holidays.
Serve it to guests with dessert on a snowy evening.

Yields about 8 cups

Cooking time: 3–4 hours
Preparation time: 15 minutes
Attention: Minimal
Pot size: 3–5 quarts

2 quarts apple cider
½ cup brown sugar
¼ teaspoon salt
1 teaspoon whole allspice
1 teaspoon whole cloves
1 3-inch stick cinnamon bark
20 whole cloves
1 orange

1. Combine the cider, brown sugar, and salt in the slow cooker.

2. Tie the allspice, 1 teaspoon cloves, and cinnamon in a small piece of cheesecloth; add to the cider.

3. Cover and heat on a low setting for 2 to 3 hours.

4. Press 20 cloves in circles around the orange. Slice the orange between the clove rings. Half an hour before serving, add the clove-studded orange slices to the slow cooker. Remove spice bundle before serving.

Family Party Punch

This nonalcoholic punch is great for the whole family.
You can also chill the leftover punch and drink it with ice.

Yields about 9 cups

Cooking time: 2–3 hours
Preparation time: 15 minutes
Attention: Minimal
Pot size: 3–5 quarts

½ large lemon
1 12-ounce can frozen orange
juice concentrate
1 12-ounce can frozen
raspberry juice
concentrate
4 cups water
3 cups lemon-lime soda
1 stick cinnamon bark
3 oranges

1. Thinly slice the lemon. Put the lemon, juice concentrates, water, soda, and cinnamon in the slow cooker.

2. Cover and heat on a low setting for 2 to 3 hours.

3. Thinly slice the oranges. Before serving, replace the lemon slices with the orange slices.

Orange Mocha

Serve this rich drink with a twist of orange peel as a garnish.
Flame the orange peel briefly to bring out the scent.

1. Combine the coffee, cocoa, and sugar in the slow cooker.

2. Cover and heat on a low setting for 2 to 3 hours.

3. Half an hour before serving, stir in the liqueurs.

4. Whip the cream and provide as a garnish for individual servings.

Yields about 9 cups

Cooking time: 3–4 hours
Preparation time: 15 minutes
Attention: Minimal
Pot size: 3–5 quarts

8 cups brewed coffee
¼ cup cocoa powder
¾ cup sugar
½ cup orange liqueur
½ cup coffee liqueur
1 cup heavy cream

Steamy Mint Malt

This is a great way to make use of leftover Halloween candy.
Turn it into a yummy hot drink.

1. Combine the candies, milk, malt powder, and vanilla in the slow cooker.

2. Cover and heat on a low setting for 2 to 3 hours.

3. Before serving, beat with a rotary mixer until frothy.

4. Whip the cream and provide as a garnish for individual servings.

Yields about 5 cups

Cooking time: 2–3 hours
Preparation time: 30 minutes
Attention: Moderate
Pot size: 3–5 quarts

6 chocolate-covered mint
   patties
6 chocolate Hershey's Kisses
5 cups milk
½ cup malted milk powder
1 teaspoon vanilla
1 cup heavy cream

Spicy Lemonade Punch

This punch is nonalcoholic, but it still has some lemony tang.
For even more vitamin C, you can use fresh lemonade instead of concentrate.

Yields about 9 cups

Cooking time: 3–4 hours
Preparation time: 2 hours
Attention: Minimal
Pot size: 3–5 quarts

1 lemon
2 sticks cinnamon bark
6 whole cloves
4 cups cranberry juice
1 12-ounce can lemonade
*   concentrate*
⅔ cup sugar
4 cups water
2 tablespoons honey

1. Slice the lemon. Break the cinnamon sticks into 1-inch pieces. Tie the cloves and cinnamon sticks in a cheesecloth bag.

2. Combine the spice bag with the cranberry juice, lemonade concentrate, sugar, water, and honey in the slow cooker.

3. Cover and heat on a low setting for 2 to 3 hours.

4. Before serving, remove the spice bag and discard. Use lemon slices as garnish for individual servings.

Hot Buttered Punch

Not many drinks these days include butter, but this treat carries
a long tradition. It's unique and yummy.

Yields about 10 cups

Cooking time: 3–4 hours
Preparation time: 15 minutes
Attention: Moderate
Pot size: 3–5 quarts

¾ cup brown sugar
4 cups water
¼ teaspoon salt
¼ teaspoon nutmeg
½ teaspoon cinnamon
½ teaspoon allspice
¾ teaspoon ground cloves
2 1-pound cans jellied
*   cranberry sauce*
1 quart pineapple juice
16 sticks cinnamon bark
16 small dabs butter

1. Combine the sugar, water, salt, spices, cranberry sauce, and pineapple juice in the slow cooker.

2. Cover and heat on a low setting for 3 to 4 hours. Stir twice to blend in the cranberry sauce as it melts.

3. Provide the cinnamon sticks and butter dabs to garnish individual servings. Keep the butter chilled, ready for guests to drop in their drink.

Beach Tea

*This delicious drink is great for soothing a cold.
You can also add some rum to this, for an extra warming effect.*

1. Thinly slice the orange.

2. Combine the orange, water, sugar, honey, and juices in the slow cooker.

3. Cover and heat on a low setting for 2 to 3 hours.

4. Half an hour before serving, add the tea bags for 10 minutes; then remove and discard the tea bags.

Yields about 9 cups

Cooking time: 3–4 hours
Preparation time: 15 minutes
Attention: Moderate
Pot size: 3–5 quarts

*1 orange
6 cups water
⅓ cup sugar
2 tablespoons honey
1½ cups orange juice
1½ cups pineapple juice
6 tea bags*

Belgian Coffee

*This is excellent after dinner, or after ice cream, and looks beautiful with
an additional garnish of fresh raspberry and a mint sprig.*

1. Grate or chop the dark chocolate.

2. Combine the coffee, liqueur, and dark chocolate in the slow cooker.

3. Cover and heat on a low setting for 2 to 3 hours.

4. Whip the cream. Provide the whipped cream and chocolate mint sticks as a garnish for individual servings.

Yields about 9 cups

Cooking time: 2–3 hours
Preparation time: 15 minutes
Attention: Minimal
Pot size: 3–5 quarts

*8 squares dark chocolate
8 cups coffee
1 cup mint liqueur
1 cup heavy cream
8 chocolate mint sticks*

Homemade Coffee Liqueur

You can also serve this chilled, over ice.
Or drizzle it over your favorite chocolate cake and let it seep in overnight.

Yields about 7 cups

Cooking time: 3–4 hours
Preparation time: 15 minutes
Attention: Minimal
Pot size: 3–5 quarts

4 cups dark coffee
3 cups sugar
5 teaspoons vanilla extract
3 cups vodka

1. Combine the coffee, sugar, and half the vanilla in the slow cooker.

2. Cover and heat on a low setting for 2 to 3 hours. Stir twice to blend in the sugar as it dissolves.

3. An hour before serving, add the remaining vanilla and the vodka.

Get with the Program

Update your slow cooker collection with a newer model that has a removable crockery pot. It simplifies preparing ahead, storage, and cleanup, plus you can pop the crockery pot in an insulated carrying case and do your entertaining on the road.

Cafe Vienna

This rich drink is even better if you use the best coffee available.
You can also substitute brown sugar or turbinado sugar.

Yields about 8 cups

Cooking time: 2–3 hours
Preparation time: 15 minutes
Attention: Minimal
Pot size: 3–5 quarts

4 squares dark chocolate
8 cups coffee
½ cup sugar
½ cup heavy cream
¼ teaspoon ground nutmeg
8 sticks cinnamon bark

1. Grate or chop the chocolate.

2. Combine the chocolate, coffee, sugar, cream, and nutmeg in the slow cooker.

3. Cover and heat on a low setting for 2 to 3 hours.

4. Provide the cinnamon sticks as garnish for individual servings.

Rosy Red Cheeks

This drink is excellent for a cold winter evening.
Add a few drops of red food coloring for extra holiday color.

1. Combine the cranberry juice, orange juice concentrate, sugar, allspice, and wine in the slow cooker.

2. Cover and heat on a low setting for 2 to 3 hours.

3. Slice the orange and stud the orange slices with the cloves. Half an hour before serving, put the orange slices in the slow cooker.

Yields about 6 cups

Cooking time: 3–4 hours
Preparation time: 15 minutes
Attention: Minimal
Pot size: 3–5 quarts

2 cups cranberry juice cocktail
1 6-ounce can frozen orange juice concentrate
1 tablespoon sugar
¼ teaspoon ground allspice
1 bottle dry red wine
1 orange
10 whole cloves

Medicinal Blackberry Cordial

This drink should be served in small glasses.
It's also excellent over vanilla ice cream or soaked into white cake.

1. Combine the blackberries, sugar, and spices in the slow cooker. Mash them together with a potato masher.

2. Add the water. Cover and heat on a low setting for 2 to 3 hours.

3. An hour before serving, add the brandy.

Yields about 8 cups

Cooking time: 3–4 hours
Preparation time: 30 minutes
Attention: Minimal
Pot size: 3–5 quarts

3 pounds blackberries
1 cup sugar
1 teaspoon cinnamon
1 teaspoon mace
1 teaspoon ground cloves
½ cup water
2 cups brandy

Sugar on Fire

This recipe will grab all your guests' attention.
Serve it when there's a lull in your party to get everyone energized again.

Yields about 8 cups

Cooking time: 2–3 hours
Preparation time: 30 minutes
Attention: Moderate
Pot size: 3–5 quarts

2 bottles dry red wine
1½ cups granulated sugar
6 whole cloves
1 cup orange juice
½ cup lemon juice
6 1-inch strips orange peel
4 1-inch strips lemon peel
1 orange
½ cup rum
½ cup sugar cubes

1. Combine the wine with the granulated sugar (not the cubes), cloves, fruit juices, and peels in the slow cooker.

2. Cover and heat on a low setting for 2 to 3 hours.

3. Slice the orange; set aside.

4. Heat the rum in a saucepan over low heat until the rum steams. Soak the sugar cubes in the rum. Place the cubes in a metal strainer or metal slotted spoon just over the punch.

5. Ignite the sugar cubes. As they flame, gradually pour the rest of the heated rum over the cubes. When the sugar has all melted into the punch, add a few orange slices.

A Slick Trick

Before measuring sticky liquids like honey and molasses, grease your measuring cup and then rinse it with hot water. The molasses will still flow slowly like...well, molasses, but you won't lose half of your measurement on the sides of the measuring cup.

Cafe Aromatica

This nonalcoholic brew is ideal for a gray winter afternoon,
or for the end of the evening, before your guests head out into a storm.

Yields about 6 cups

Cooking time: 2–3 hours
Preparation time: 15 minutes
Attention: Minimal
Pot size: 3–5 quarts

1. Peel and slice the oranges, and cut ½ cup of the peel into very thin strips.

2. Combine the coffee, orange slices, ½ cup peel strips, sugar, and bitters in the slow cooker.

3. Cover and heat on a low setting for 2 to 3 hours.

4. Whip the cream and provide as a garnish for individual servings.

2 oranges
6 cups double-strength coffee
¼ cup sugar
2 teaspoons aromatic bitters
1 cup heavy cream.

Aunt Ellie's Spiced Grape Tea

This is a good drink to be sipping indoors with friends on a rainy day.
Try using white grape juice in this recipe.

Yields about 10 cups

Cooking time: 2–3 hours
Preparation time: 15 minutes
Attention: Minimal
Pot size: 3–5 quarts

1. Put the cinnamon, tea, and cloves in a loose cloth bag.

2. Combine the spice bag with the grape juice, sugar, and water in the slow cooker.

3. Cover and heat on a low setting for 2 to 3 hours.

4. Before serving, remove the cloth bag.

3 sticks cinnamon bark
¼ cup loose tea
10 cloves
3 cups grape juice
½ cup sugar
7 cups water

Ginger Punch

This punch is not only delicious, but it's also good for you.
Fresh ginger has healthful effects.

Yields about 10 cups

Cooking time: 3–4 hours
Preparation time: 15 minutes
Attention: Minimal
Pot size: 3–5 quarts

1 inch fresh gingerroot
1 cup sugar
8 cups water
6 cloves
1 stick cinnamon bark
½ cup lemon juice
1½ cups orange juice
1 sprig mint

1. Peel and mince the gingerroot.

2. Put the ginger, sugar, water, cloves, and cinnamon in the slow cooker.

3. Cover and heat on a low setting for 2 to 3 hours.

4. An hour before serving, add the fruit juices and the mint.

Be Prepared
Make a few dishes ahead of time and keep them in plastic containers in the freezer. On the morning of party day, line up the slow cookers, pop in your frozen delicacies, turn the heat on low, and when you get back from work you'll be ready to go.

Spicy Sunday Tea

This aromatic tea will not only give your home a lovely scent while you cook it, but it will also warm you up on the inside.

Yields about 9 cups

Cooking time: 3–4 hours
Preparation time: 30 minutes
Attention: Moderate
Pot size: 3–5 quarts

¼ teaspoon cinnamon
¼ teaspoon whole cloves
6 teaspoons tea
8 cups water
1 cup sugar
1 lemon
2 oranges

1. Tie the cinnamon, cloves, and tea in a loose cloth bag. Place the bag in the slow cooker.

2. Boil 2 cups of the water. Pour it over the spice bag in the slow cooker and let this steep 5 minutes.

3. Add the remaining water and sugar to the slow cooker. Cover and heat on a low setting for 2 to 3 hours.

4. Extract the juice from the lemon and oranges. Half an hour before serving, remove the spice bag and add the juices.

Step One: Make a List
The first thing you should do is make a list of all the preparations you need for your party. List ingredients, decorations, cookware, and anything else you might need. Check off the boxes as you go, and on party day, take joy in throwing the list away.

Aunt Ellie's Spiced Grape Juice

*This hot drink is better if made the day before,
left overnight in a cool place, then reheated and served.*

Yields about 12 cups

Cooking time: 2–3 hours
Preparation time: 15 minutes
Attention: Minimal
Pot size: 3–5 quarts

12 1-inch sticks cinnamon
    bark
12 whole cloves
12 cups grape juice
½ cup sugar
⅛ teaspoon salt
¼ cup lemon juice

1. Tie the cinnamon and cloves in a cloth bag.

2. Combine the spice bag with the grape juice, sugar, and salt in the slow cooker.

3. Cover and heat on a low setting for 2 to 3 hours.

4. Before serving, remove the cloth bag and add the lemon juice.

Maturation

Slow cooking allows flavors to mature, meaning they actually go through chemical changes that simply take time. This happens in other slow systems that use time as an asset, such as the aging of wine and cheese.

chapter 15
cakes and puddings

Leftover Cake Pudding

Yields 1 loaf

Cooking time: 2–3 hours
Preparation time: 30 minutes
Attention: Minimal
Pot size: 3–5 quarts

3 cups cubed leftover cake
¼ pound raisins
3 eggs
¼ cup sugar
2 cups milk
¼ teaspoon nutmeg
½ teaspoon vanilla

When made with white cake, this dish is irresistible with Brandy Sauce (page 44). Stockpile leftover cake in the freezer until you have enough.

1. Pile the cake cubes in a greased and floured loaf pan or the equivalent. Sprinkle with the raisins.

2. Beat the eggs; add the sugar, milk, nutmeg, and vanilla to the eggs. Pour the egg mixture over the cake pieces and raisins.

3. Loosely cover the dish with foil or other lid. Place on a trivet or rack in the slow cooker, and pour water around the base of the trivet.

4. Cover and heat on a high setting for 2 to 3 hours.

Stale Cake
Don't think of it as stale, think of it as highly absorbent. Leftover cake gives you an excuse to make a delicious dessert sauce. Use cake leftover from birthday parties or holidays—a chocolate cake, a fruited one, or a combination of more than one kind. Stack together cake squares and dip away.

Tropical Rice Pudding

Drizzle a few spoonfuls of warm Coconut Milk (page 193)
over the top for a delicious taste. This can be served hot or cold.

Yields 1 loaf

Cooking time: 2–3 hours
Preparation time: 30 minutes
Attention: Minimal
Pot size: 3–5 quarts

1 can evaporated milk
1 cup water
2 eggs
½ cup sugar
1 teaspoon vanilla
¼ teaspoon salt
1 teaspoon nutmeg
¼ teaspoon allspice
2 cups cooked rice
¾ cup shredded coconut

1. Mix the evaporated milk, water, eggs, sugar, vanilla, salt, and spices.

2. Combine the rice and coconut and put in a greased and floured loaf pan or the equivalent.

3. Pour the milk mixture over the rice.

4. Loosely cover the dish with foil or other lid. Place on a trivet or rack in the slow cooker, and pour water around the base of the trivet.

5. Cover and heat on a high setting for 2 to 3 hours.

Chocolate Potato Cake

Yes, you can convert those leftover mashed potatoes into something worth raiding the refrigerator for. Skip the gravy, though.

Yields 2 loaves

Cooking time: 2–3 hours
Preparation time: 45 minutes
Attention: Minimal
Pot size: 3–5 quarts

¾ cup butter
2¼ cups sugar
1 cup mashed potatoes
3 eggs
1¾ cups flour
2 teaspoons baking powder
1 teaspoon salt
½ teaspoon cream of tartar
½ teaspoon ground cloves
½ teaspoon ground nutmeg
1½ teaspoons ground
   cinnamon
½ cup milk
2 ounces unsweetened
   chocolate

1. Cream the butter and sugar in a mixing bowl; blend in the potatoes, then the eggs.

2. Sift the flour with the baking powder, salt, cream of tartar, and spices.

3. Add the dry mixture and the milk gradually to the potato mixture. Keep blending well. Grate the chocolate and add.

4. Fill 2 greased and floured loaf pans, or the equivalent, one-half to three-quarters full with the batter. Loosely cover each dish with foil or other lid. Place on a trivet or rack in the slow cooker, and pour water around the base of the trivet.

5. Cover and heat on a high setting for 2 to 3 hours.

Calling All Chocolate Lovers

Are you a chocolate fiend? Get some of your favorite chocolates and tuck them into the batter of your cake, pudding, or bread. The chocolates will melt and transform as your concoction cooks.

Apple Coconut Cake

The coconut gives this cake a nice texture. This goes well with Banana Sauce Flambé (page 43) or Tangiers Orange Sauce (page 46).

Yields 2 loaves

Cooking time: 2–3 hours
Preparation time: 45 minutes
Attention: Minimal
Pot size: 3–5 quarts

*4 cups apples, peeled, cored,
   and chopped*
2 cups sugar
3 cups flour
2 teaspoons baking soda
1 teaspoon salt
1 cup vegetable oil
2 eggs
1 teaspoon vanilla
1 cup chopped nuts
1 cup shredded coconut

1. Mix the apples with the sugar and let stand until juice develops.

2. Sift together the dry ingredients and add to the apple mixture. Add the oil, eggs, vanilla, nuts, and coconut to this and mix well.

3. Fill 2 greased and floured loaf pans, or the equivalent, one-half to three-quarters full with the batter. Loosely cover each dish with foil or other lid. Place on a trivet or rack in the slow cooker, and pour water around the base of the trivet.

4. Cover and heat on a high setting for 2 to 3 hours.

Condensation Tip

When steaming cakes, breads, or puddings, use a small bit of foil to prop open the lid enough to let some steam escape. This will cut down on condensation on the lid, which could drop back down onto your baked goods.

Chocolate Pound Cake

Serve this cake with hot fudge sauce and vanilla ice cream.
Add whipped cream and a cherry to make a pound cake sundae.

Yields 1 loaf

Cooking time: 2–3 hours
Preparation time: 45 minutes
Attention: Minimal
Pot size: 3–5 quarts

½ pound butter
½ cup shortening
2¾ cups sugar
5 eggs
1 tablespoon vanilla
3 cups flour
5 tablespoons cocoa powder
½ teaspoon baking powder
½ teaspoon salt
1 cup milk

1. Cream the butter, shortening, and sugar. Stir in the eggs and vanilla.

2. Sift the flour with the cocoa powder, baking powder, and salt.

3. Mix all the ingredients, alternating between adding the dry ingredients and the milk to the creamed mixture.

4. Fill 1 greased and floured loaf pan, or the equivalent, one-half to three-quarters full with the batter. Loosely cover with foil or other lid. Place on a trivet or rack in the slow cooker, and pour water around the base of the trivet.

5. Cover and heat on a high setting for 2 to 3 hours.

Samantha's Bubbly Cake

This is a fun cake to make with children.
They'll enjoy pouring a can of soda pop into the mixing bowl.

1. Cream the butter, shortening, and sugar. Add the egg and mix well.

2. In a separate bowl, mix the vanilla, lemon juice, and soda pop.

3. Alternate adding the flour and liquid ingredients to the creamed mixture.

4. Fill 2 greased and floured loaf pans, or the equivalent, one-half to three-quarters full with the batter. Loosely cover each dish with foil or other lid. Place on a trivet or rack in the slow cooker, and pour water around the base of the trivet.

5. Cover and heat on a high setting for 2 to 3 hours.

Flour Power
Not all flours are alike. Cake flour is made from a variety of wheat that can be ground into smaller particles. All-purpose flour is made from a mixture of wheat varieties, adequate for cake but also suitable for bread.

Yields 2 loaves

Cooking time: 2–3 hours
Preparation time: 30 minutes
Attention: Minimal
Pot size: 3–5 quarts

½ cup butter
½ cup shortening
2 cups sugar
1 egg
1 teaspoon vanilla
1 teaspoon lemon juice
7 ounces lemon-lime soda pop
3 cups flour

Avocado Cake

Top this cake with a dusting of powdered sugar.
And don't tell your guests there's avocado in it until they've taken a bite.

Yields 2 loaves

Cooking time: 2–3 hours
Preparation time: 45 minutes
Attention: Minimal
Pot size: 3–5 quarts

¾ cup butter
2 cups sugar
3 eggs
2 avocados
2⅔ cups cake flour
¾ teaspoon cinnamon
¾ teaspoon allspice
¾ teaspoon salt
1½ teaspoons baking soda
¾ cup buttermilk
⅓ cup dates
¾ cup nuts
¾ cup white raisins

1. Cream the butter and sugar. Add the eggs and mix well. Dice and mix in the avocado.

2. Sift the flour, spices, and salt together. Dissolve the baking soda in the buttermilk.

3. Add the buttermilk and sifted ingredients to the creamed mixture, alternating between adding wet and dry. Mix well. Pit and chop the dates. Chop the nuts. Fold in the dates, raisins, and nuts.

4. Fill 2 greased and floured loaf pans, or the equivalent, one-half to three-quarters full with the batter. Loosely cover each dish with foil or other lid. Place on a trivet or rack in the slow cooker, and pour water around the base of the trivet.

5. Cover and heat on a high setting for 2 to 3 hours.

Stay Afloat

To keep fruits and nuts from sinking to the bottom of a cake, heat the chopped fruits and nuts for 5 minutes in a 250°F oven, then shake in a paper or plastic bag with flour before adding to your batter.

Cinnamon Pear Cake

Serve this cake warm.
Use fresh sliced pears or Wild Vanilla Sauce (page 47) as a topping.

1. Mix the oil, sugar, eggs, and vanilla.

2. Sift the flour, salt, baking soda, and cinnamon together. Add to the egg mixture.

3. Core and dice the pears; chop the pecans. Fold the pears and pecans into the batter.

4. Fill 2 greased and floured loaf pans, or the equivalent, one-half to three-quarters full with the batter. Loosely cover each dish with foil or other lid. Place on a trivet or rack in the slow cooker, and pour water around the base of the trivet.

5. Cover and heat on a high setting for 2 to 3 hours.

Whip Tip

Homemade whipped cream is much better than store-bought, so make your own instead! One tip is to prechill the mixing bowl and the beaters to be used. Also, add flavors. For each cup of whipping cream, beat in a tablespoon of cocoa powder and 2 teaspoons of sugar, or a tablespoon of liqueur, ¼ teaspoon almond extract, or ¼ teaspoon minced citrus peel.

Yields 2 loaves

Cooking time: 2–3 hours
Preparation time: 45 minutes
Attention: Minimal
Pot size: 3–5 quarts

1½ cups vegetable oil
2 cups sugar
3 eggs
1 teaspoon vanilla
3 cups sifted flour
¾ teaspoon salt
1 teaspoon baking soda
1 teaspoon cinnamon
2 pears
1 cup pecans

Spicy Molasses Cake

*This cake is delicious served warm with a cup of coffee
and a scoop of vanilla ice cream on the side.*

Yields 3 loaves

Cooking time: 2–3 hours
Preparation time: 45 minutes
Attention: Minimal
Pot size: 3–5 quarts

1 cup shortening
1 cup sugar
2 eggs
1 cup molasses
4½ cups flour
6 teaspoons baking powder
½ teaspoon baking soda
1 teaspoon salt
1 teaspoon allspice
1 teaspoon cinnamon
1 cup sour milk
1 cup raisins

1. Cream the shortening and sugar until fluffy. Add the eggs and mix well, then add the molasses and mix well.

2. Sift the flour with the baking powder, baking soda, salt, and spices. Alternately add the dry mixture and the milk to the creamed mixture. Fold in the raisins.

3. Fill 3 greased and floured loaf pans, or the equivalent, one-half to three-quarters full with the batter. Loosely cover each dish with foil or other lid. Place on a trivet or rack in the slow cooker, and pour water around the base of the trivet.

4. Cover and heat on a high setting for 2 to 3 hours.

Cutting the Cake

For nice, professional-looking slices, freeze cakes before cutting. As a bonus, cold cake is excellent with ice cream on a hot day. Or serve your cold cakes with a hot sauce, giving a nice contrast.

Lemony Apple Pudding

The combination of lemon rinds and mace gives this cake a nice zing. This is excellent with cinnamon-laced whipped cream or lemon sherbet.

Yields 2 loaves

Cooking time: 2–3 hours
Preparation time: 45 minutes
Attention: Minimal
Pot size: 3–5 quarts

1 cup butter
1 cup sugar
8 eggs
1 cup milk
3 cups flour
1 tablespoon baking powder
2 lemon rinds
4 apples
⅛ teaspoon mace

1. Cream the butter and sugar, then add the eggs and milk.

2. Sift the flour and baking powder together, then add to the liquid mixture.

3. Grate the rinds; peel, core, and dice the apples. Add the rinds, apples, and mace to the other ingredients.

4. Fill 2 greased and floured loaf pans, or the equivalent, one-half to three-quarters full with the batter. Loosely cover each dish with foil or other lid. Place on a trivet or rack in the slow cooker, and pour water around the base of the trivet.

5. Cover and heat on a high setting for 2 to 3 hours.

Whip It
You can freeze whipped cream. Make a big batch early, then spoon individual servings onto waxed paper and pop it into the freezer. When firm, move the frozen servings to a sealed container. Later, put each on a dessert, or a dessert drink, and it's ready to serve in minutes.

Flaming Plum Pudding

Warm some brandy until it steams, heat the pudding,
sprinkle with powdered sugar, drizzle with hot brandy, and light.

Yields 3 loaves

Cooking time: 2–3 hours
Preparation time: 60 minutes
Attention: Minimal
Pot size: 3–5 quarts

2 cups shortening
2 cups brown sugar
4 eggs
1 cup molasses
1 cup brandy
2 lemons
2 cups flour
½ teaspoon nutmeg
½ teaspoon ground ginger
½ teaspoon ground cloves
½ teaspoon cinnamon
½ pound orange peel
½ pound lemon peel
1 cup bread crumbs
1 pound currants
½ pound golden raisins

1. Cream the shortening and the sugar. Add the eggs, molasses, and brandy. Squeeze the lemons and add the lemon juice.

2. Sift the flour with the spices. Mince the orange and lemon peel. Mix the minced peel, crumbs, currants, and raisins together. Stir this into the dry ingredients.

3. Combine the ingredients, stirring the dry ingredients into the liquid mixture.

4. Fill 3 greased and floured loaf pans, or the equivalent, one-half to three-quarters full with the batter. Loosely cover each dish with foil or other lid. Place on a trivet or rack in the slow cooker, and pour water around the base of the trivet.

5. Cover and heat on a high setting for 2 to 3 hours.

The Meaning of Pudding
In a slow cooker, pudding is different from the standard kind you find in a box. A "pudding" is traditionally a steamed sweet bread, like the well-known plum pudding, and is also a general term for a sweet that follows the evening meal.

Bread Pudding au Chocolat

Save your bread loaf ends and stale slices in a resealable container in the freezer. As soon as you have enough, use them in this recipe.

Yields 1 loaf

Cooking time: 2–3 hours
Preparation time: 45 minutes
Attention: Minimal
Pot size: 3–5 quarts

¼ cup butter
3 cups cubed dry bread
¾ cup sugar
2 teaspoons vanilla
2 eggs
2 cups milk
½ cup semisweet chocolate, grated
¼ cup unsweetened cocoa powder
½ teaspoon ground cinnamon

1. Use half of the butter to grease a loaf pan or the equivalent. Add the bread cubes to the pan.

2. Cream the remaining butter and sugar. Add vanilla, eggs, and milk.

3. Grate the chocolate into thick flakes. Stir the chocolate, cocoa powder, and cinnamon into the milk mixture.

4. Pour the milk mixture over the bread cubes. Loosely cover the dish with foil or other lid. Place on a trivet or rack in the slow cooker, and pour water around the base of the trivet.

5. Cover and heat on a high setting for 2 to 3 hours.

Bread Pudding Options
When making bread pudding, use a mixture of breads. Try French baguettes, strong pumpernickel, or sweet raisin bread. The more stale and dry they are, the more sweet custard they'll absorb while cooking.

Apple Ring Pudding

*Top this with whipped cream and a sprinkle of cinnamon.
Serve with Hot Mulled Cider (page 214) for a complete dessert.*

Yields 1 loaf

Cooking time: 2–3 hours
Preparation time: 30 minutes
Attention: Minimal
Pot size: 3–5 quarts

6 tablespoons butter
6 apples
¾ cup sugar
½ cup water
¾ cup flour
1 teaspoon cinnamon

1. Use one-third of the butter to butter a loaf pan or the equivalent. Peel and core the apples, then slice crosswise and layer in the pan.

2. Cream the remaining butter with the sugar. Stir in the water. Sift the flour with the cinnamon and combine with the creamed mixture.

3. Spread the batter over the apples.

4. Loosely cover the baking dish with foil or other lid. Place on a trivet or rack in the slow cooker, and pour water around the base of the trivet.

5. Cover and heat on a high setting for 2 to 3 hours.

Slow and Spicy
Extended cooking develops strong flavors from spices. When converting recipes, cut the amount of spices added in half until you have tested it once, especially if you are using fresh spices instead of dried ones.

Northern Date Pudding

You can substitute any nut for pecans. Try hazelnuts or macadamias, for example, roasted first, then coarsely chopped.

Yields 1 loaf

Cooking time: 2–3 hours
Preparation time: 45 minutes
Attention: Minimal
Pot size: 3–5 quarts

1 cup dates
1 cup brown sugar
½ cup milk
1½ cups flour
2 teaspoons baking powder
¼ teaspoon salt
¼ cup chopped pecans
2½ cups water
2 cups brown sugar
2 tablespoons butter

1. Pit and chop the dates and mix with 1 cup brown sugar. Add the milk.

2. Sift the flour with the baking powder and salt. Add to the dates. Stir in the nuts. Spread the mixture in a greased and floured loaf pan or the equivalent.

3. Boil the water. Add the remaining 2 cups of brown sugar and the butter. Pour the liquid over the top of the flour-and-date mixture in the pan.

4. Loosely cover the dish with foil or other lid. Place on a trivet or rack in the slow cooker, and pour water around the base of the trivet.

5. Cover and heat on a high setting for 2 to 3 hours.

Cracking Pecans
Do you need whole pecans for your recipe? Pour boiling water over the pecan shells and let them stand 10 minutes. Then dry and crack carefully, and the pecan meats should come out whole.

Sweet Cranberry Pudding

This recipe sweetens bitter cranberries to make a tangy treat.
Serve warm with a dollop of whipped cream.

Yields 1 loaf

Cooking time: 2–3 hours
Preparation time: 15 minutes
Attention: Minimal
Pot size: 3–5 quarts

1⅓ cups flour
⅛ teaspoon salt
2 teaspoons baking soda
2 cups whole fresh
 cranberries
¼ cup molasses
¼ cup corn syrup
¼ cup water

1. Sift the flour with the salt and baking soda. Stir in the cranberries.

2. Mix the molasses, corn syrup, and water. Add to the dry ingredients.

3. Fill a greased and floured loaf pan, or the equivalent, one-half to three-quarters full with the batter. Loosely cover the dish with foil or other lid. Place on a trivet or rack in the slow cooker, and pour water around the base of the trivet.

4. Cover and heat on a high setting for 2 to 3 hours.

Perfect Timing

Using combinations of timers and frozen ingredients means a slow cooker can be set out and scheduled to start cooking while you sleep. Even if you don't have a timer, you can freeze some of the ingredients, such as the broth or browned meat, before you put them into the slow cooker at bedtime. This will slow down the cooking, reducing the effective cooking time.

chapter 16
fruit

Apricots in Brandy

*Try using a small round cookie cutter to cut your apricots
for an attractive presentation.*

Yields about 5 cups

Cooking time: 4–5 hours
Preparation time: 15 minutes
Attention: Moderate
Pot size: 3–5 quarts

*2 pounds dried apricots
3 cups water
2 cups sugar
1 cup brandy*

1. Halve the apricots with kitchen shears. Combine the apricots, water, and sugar in the slow cooker.

2. Cover and heat on a low setting for 3 to 4 hours. Stir once after the first hour to distribute the sugar.

3. An hour before serving, add the brandy.

Cutting Dried Fruit

Dip a clean pair of kitchen shears in hot water when cutting dried apricots, peaches, or other fruits. Chilling the fruit also helps, keeping them stiffer; the difference in temperature helps the blade cut more smoothly.

Holiday Fruit

You can peel the apples if you wish, but it's not necessary.
And if you want to substitute other nuts for walnuts, pecans work well.

Serves 6
_____

Cooking time: 4–5 hours
Preparation time: 30 minutes
Attention: Minimal
Pot size: 3–5 quarts

1. Grate the peel from the lemon section. Pit and chop the dates. Core and slice the apples.

2. Combine the grated peel, dates, apples, wine, butter, sugar, spices, and cranberries in the slow cooker.

3. Cover and heat on a low setting for 3 to 4 hours.

4. Chop the walnuts. Half an hour before serving, add the walnuts.

5. Provide sour cream for garnishing individual servings.

¼ lemon
½ cup dates
4 apples
½ cup port wine
1 tablespoon butter
1¼ cups sugar
⅛ teaspoon cinnamon
⅛ teaspoon nutmeg
2 cups fresh cranberries
⅓ cup walnuts
1 cup sour cream

Fruit Emergency!

If you run out of fresh fruit, you can sometimes use dried fruit (plus a little extra liquid) in slow-cooker recipes. Don't be shy. Use those strange fruits or trail mixes buried in the back of your cupboard. You might find a winning combination.

Figs in Cognac

These figs are sensational over ice cream.
You can also serve them on plain white cake or ladyfingers.

Yields about 5 cups

Cooking time: 4–5 hours
Preparation time: 15 minutes
Attention: Minimal
Pot size: 3–5 quarts

2 pounds dried figs
3 cups water
2 cups sugar
1 cup cognac

1. Halve the figs with kitchen shears. Combine the figs, water, and sugar in the slow cooker.

2. Cover and heat on a low setting for 3 to 4 hours. Stir once after the first hour to distribute the sugar.

3. An hour before serving, add the cognac.

Baked Apples

Score each skin with a grid of cuts.
This will make it easy for your guests to pull apart the baked apples.

Serves 6

Cooking time: 3–4 hours
Preparation time: 30 minutes
Attention: Minimal
Pot size: 3–5 quarts

½ cup dates
6 baking apples
¼ cup butter
30 whole cloves
1 cup water
1 cup brown sugar
½ teaspoon ground cinnamon
¼ teaspoon ground nutmeg

1. Pit and chop the dates; core the apples. Fill the centers of the apples with dates and a few dabs of butter. Press several cloves into each apple.

2. Arrange the apples in the slow cooker.

3. Mix the water, brown sugar, spices, and remaining cloves. Pour the mixture over the apples.

4. Cover and heat on a low setting for 3 to 4 hours.

Grown-Up Apple Sauce

This is not the apple sauce you ate from baby food jars!
This is delicious by itself or on ice cream.

Serves 4–6

Cooking time: 3–4 hours
Preparation time: 15 minutes
Attention: Minimal
Pot size: 3–5 quarts

6 apples
1 cup white wine
¼ cup water
1 tablespoon butter
2 tablespoons brown sugar
1 1-inch stick cinnamon bark

1. Core and cube the apples, but don't peel them.

2. Combine the apples, wine, water, butter, sugar, and cinnamon in the slow cooker.

3. Cover and heat on low setting for 3 to 4 hours.

Choosing Your Apples

Not all apples are alike. You may have been disappointed by the pasty flavor or mealy texture of a beautiful apple after baking. If so, it was probably bred for looks, not taste. Try Rome, McIntosh, and Jonathan apples, which are commonly available and were bred for good cooking.

Honey Rhubarb Sauce

This sweet sauce is delicious over virtually anything.
Try it on cake, ice cream, or sweet bread.

Yields about 6–7 cups

Cooking time: 3–4 hours
Preparation time: 15 minutes
Attention: Minimal
Pot size: 3–5 quarts

4 pounds rhubarb
2 sticks cinnamon bark
1 cup sugar
½ cup honey
2 cups water

1. Cut the rhubarb in 2-inch pieces, discarding the leaves and the bases of the stalks. Leave the cinnamon sticks intact.

2. Combine the rhubarb, cinnamon, sugar, honey, and water in the slow cooker.

3. Cover and heat on a low setting for 3 to 4 hours.

Dried Fruit Compote

What dried fruits do you have available? Try substituting them
in this recipe and see what combinations your guests like.

Yields about 6 cups

Cooking time: 4–5 hours
Preparation time: 15 minutes
Attention: Minimal
Pot size: 3–5 quarts

½ lemon
½ pound dried apricots
½ pound dried figs
½ pound prunes
½ pound dried pitted cherries
4 cups water
1½ cups sugar
⅔ cup bourbon
1 cup heavy cream

1. Thinly slice the lemon. Halve the apricots and figs with kitchen shears. Pierce the prunes with a fork so they don't burst.

2. Combine the lemon, dried fruits, water, and sugar in the slow cooker.

3. Cover and heat on a low setting for 3 to 4 hours.

4. An hour before serving, add the bourbon.

5. Whip the cream and provide as a garnish for individual servings.

Vanilla Plums

For a delicious twist, replace some of the water in this recipe with wine.
The alcohol will burn off during cooking.

Serves 6–8

Cooking time: 3–4 hours
Preparation time: 15 minutes
Attention: Minimal
Pot size: 3–5 quarts

24 large ripe plums
1 cup water
1 cup white sugar
½ vanilla bean pod

1. Prick the plums all over with fork tines. Slice the plums into 8 sections. Cut through to the pits without releasing the slices from the pits.

2. Arrange the plums in the slow cooker. Add the water, then sprinkle with the sugar. Distribute segments of the vanilla bean pod in the liquid.

3. Cover and heat on a low setting for 3 to 4 hours.

Simple Can Be Good

A decadent serving of cake or ice cream lacquered with dessert sauces is perfect—sometimes. Other times, like after filling meals, a small dish, a simple spoonful of spiced fruit, and a good dark coffee are all your guests will want after your dinner party.

Baked Pears

Garnish with mint leaves. Freeze any leftover pear sauce in ice cube trays, and use the cubes to spice up your iced tea.

Serves 12

Cooking time: 3–4 hours
Preparation time: 30 minutes
Attention: Minimal
Pot size: 3–5 quarts

12 fresh pears
1 cup white raisins
3 tablespoons butter
1 cup water
½ cup sugar
½ cup honey

1. Core and peel the pears but leave the stems on, just for looks.

2. Stuff the pears from the bottom with the white raisins and a few dabs of butter.

3. Arrange the pears in the slow cooker. Add the water. Sprinkle the pears with the sugar, then drizzle with the honey.

4. Cover and heat on a low setting for 3 to 4 hours.

Baked Peaches

Serve this simple fruit with fresh mint leaves as a bright garnish. Freeze any extras to use with future desserts.

Serves 12

Cooking time: 3–4 hours
Preparation time: 15 minutes
Attention: Minimal
Pot size: 3–5 quarts

12 fresh peaches
1 cup water
½ cup brown sugar
½ cup honey

1. Prick the peaches all over with fork tines. Slice the peaches into 8 sections. Cut through to the pits without releasing the slices from the pits.

2. Arrange in the slow cooker. Add the water, then sprinkle with the sugar and drizzle with the honey.

3. Cover and heat on a low setting for 3 to 4 hours.

Steamy Dried Fruit

*Use this fruit to dress up a simple bowl of vanilla ice cream
or a piece of fluffy white cake.*

Yields about 4 cups

Cooking time: 3–4 hours
Preparation time: 15 minutes
Attention: Minimal
Pot size: 3–5 quarts

½ lemon
1½ cups dried apricots
1½ cups dried apples
½ cup dried cherries
2 cups white grape juice
3 tablespoons honey
*2 teaspoons ground anise
  seed*
1 teaspoon ground cinnamon

1. Grate the rind of the lemon. Halve the apricots and apples.

2. Combine the rind, dried fruit, juice, honey, and spices in the slow cooker.

3. Cover and heat on a low setting for 3 to 4 hours.

Protection Against Browning

After peeling sweet potatoes or apples, immediately put them in cold water with a bit of salt to prevent discoloration. The starches in the potatoes and apples react with the air, producing the color, but if they're protected with water, this won't occur.

Spiced Sweet Apples

*This works best with good baking apples, like Rome or McIntosh.
You can also use a combination of apples in all colors.*

Serves 6–8

Cooking time: 3–4 hours
Preparation time: 15 minutes
Attention: Minimal
Pot size: 3–5 quarts

12 apples
½ cup dried cherries
2 cups sugar
2 cups vinegar
12 whole cloves
1 stick cinnamon bark

1. Core, halve, and pierce the apples, scoring the skin with a knife to make it easier to pull apart later.

2. Combine the fruit, sugar, vinegar, and spices in the slow cooker.

3. Cover and heat on a low setting for 3 to 4 hours.

Peaches with Brandy Sauce

*Peeling the peaches takes time, but it makes this dish much more decadent.
Briefly dip the peaches in boiling water to aid the peeling.*

Serves 6–8

Cooking time: 3–4 hours
Preparation time: 30 minutes
Attention: Minimal
Pot size: 3–5 quarts

8 peaches
1 cup sugar
4 sprigs fresh mint
½ cup water
1 cup brandy

1. Peel, quarter, and pit the peaches.

2. Arrange the peaches in the slow cooker. Sprinkle with the sugar and mint, then add the water.

3. Cover and heat on a low setting for 2 to 3 hours.

4. An hour before serving, add the brandy.

Rosy Cranberry Bananas

*You can substitute dried apricots for cranberries,
but in that case don't add the sugar.*

Serves 10

Cooking time: 3–4 hours
Preparation time: 15 minutes
Attention: Minimal
Pot size: 3–5 quarts

2 cups fresh cranberries
10 bananas
1 cup sugar
½ cup water

1. Wash the cranberries; peel the bananas but leave them whole.

2. Arrange the bananas and cranberries in the slow cooker. Sprinkle with the sugar, then add the water.

3. Cover and heat on a low setting for 3 to 4 hours.

Spiced Cherries

Get pitted cherries, or pit them yourself. Otherwise, just warn your guests about the pits and be sure they have some place to put them.

1. Combine the cherries, sugar, vinegar, and spices in the slow cooker.

2. Cover and heat on a low setting for 3 to 4 hours. Stir at least once to distribute the sugar.

Serves 12–15

Cooking time: 3–4 hours
Preparation time: 15 minutes
Attention: Moderate
Pot size: 3–5 quarts

9 pounds fresh cherries
4 pounds sugar
1 cup cider vinegar
3 sticks cinnamon bark
1 tablespoon whole cloves

Pears Poached in Amaretto and Vanilla

These pears will make it easy to eat your recommended five servings of fruit every day, especially if you eat them over ice cream.

1. Core and halve the pears. Arrange the pears in the slow cooker.

2. Grate the peel of the lemon.

3. Sprinkle the pears with the grated peel, sugar, and vanilla. Add the Amaretto and wine.

4. Cover and heat on a low setting for 3 to 4 hours. Turn the pears twice.

Serves 12

Cooking time: 3–4 hours
Preparation time: 30 minutes
Attention: Moderate
Pot size: 3–5 quarts

12 ripe pears
½ lemon
1½ cups sugar
1 teaspoon vanilla extract
1 cup Amaretto
1 cup white wine

Sweet Rhubarb Bananas

This is delicious by itself or with a dish of ice cream.
Also try serving it with small butter cookies for dipping.

Cooking time: 3–4 hours
Preparation time: 30 minutes
Attention: Minimal
Pot size: 3–5 quarts

8 stalks rhubarb
6 bananas
¼ cup water
1 cup sugar
¼ cup butter
¼ teaspoon salt

1. Cut the rhubarb into 2-inch pieces. Slice the bananas in half lengthwise.

2. Layer half of the rhubarb and half of the bananas in the slow cooker. Add the water, and sprinkle the fruit with half of the sugar. Add the rest of the rhubarb, bananas, and sugar, in that order. Dot the fruit with the butter and sprinkle with the salt.

3. Cover and heat on a low setting for 3 to 4 hours.

Using Overripe Bananas

Do you have some overripe bananas in the house? Peel and freeze them, mushy as they are. Use them later for cooking. The riper they are, the sweeter they will be, and cooking will make any bruising undetectable. Use them in compotes, breads, curries, and hot breakfast cereals.

chapter 17
holidays and celebrations

J. D.'s Glogg

The heavenly scent of this brew will put you in a devilish party mood!
Seal the lid until you are ready to flame this Glogg.

Serves 15–20

Cooking time: 3–4 hours
Preparation time: 30 minutes
Attention: Moderate
Pot size: 5 quarts

4 cardamom pods
3 ½-inch sticks cinnamon bark
3 whole cloves
1 cup water
1 teaspoon sugar
6 prunes
½ gallon port
2 cups bourbon
½ cup raisins
½ cup blanched almonds
⅓ cup sugar
½ pint rum

1. Tie the cardamom, cinnamon, and cloves in a cheesecloth bag. Boil the spices, water, and sugar in a covered saucepan over high heat for 1 minute.

2. Pierce the prunes. Combine prunes, spice-and-water mixture, and other ingredients, except rum, in the slow cooker.

3. Cover and heat on a low setting for 3 to 4 hours.

4. Remove the spice bag. Just before serving, slowly add the rum. Light it and stand back!

Slow Glogg

This hot drink has a rich texture from the unfiltered apple juice.
Try to get freshly pressed apple juice, which is more available in the autumn.

1. Remove the seeds from the cardamom buds. Break the cinnamon sticks. Combine cardamom seeds, cinnamon sticks, cloves, nutmeg, juice, and raisins and refrigerate for 12 to 24 hours.

2. Quarter the oranges. Combine the juice mixture with orange quarters, rum, and brandy in the slow cooker.

3. Cover and heat on a low setting for 3 to 4 hours.

Serves 30–40

Cooking time: 3–4 hours
Preparation time: 15 minutes
Attention: Minimal
Pot size: 5 quarts

4 cardamom pods
3 sticks cinnamon bark
1 tablespoon whole cloves
⅛ teaspoon ground nutmeg
2 quarts unfiltered apple juice
½ pound white raisins
2 oranges
1 fifth dark rum
1 fifth brandy

Mediterranean Coffee

Be sure to provide this treat for the designated drivers at your party.
It will help everyone stay awake and interested, even into the late hours.

1. Combine the coffee, chocolate syrup, honey, and spices in the slow cooker.

2. Cover and heat on a low setting for 3 to 4 hours.

3. Peel the orange and lemon; cut the peel into thin strips. Provide the citrus strips and whipped cream to garnish each serving. Reserve the rest of the orange and the lemon for another recipe.

Serves 16

Cooking time: 3–4 hours
Preparation time: 30 minutes
Attention: Minimal
Pot size: 4–5 quarts

2 quarts strong coffee
¼ cup chocolate syrup
¼ cup honey
4 sticks cinnamon bark
1½ teaspoons whole cloves
2 anise stars
1 orange
1 lemon
1 cup whipped cream

Parsley Crab Gumbo

*You can buy fish stock and supplement it with clam juice
to make the fish broth or make your own.*

Serves 10–12

Cooking time: 4–6 hours
Preparation time: 45 minutes
Attention: Minimal
Pot size: 3–5 quarts

1 onion
1 green pepper
2 tablespoons butter
3 tomatoes
1 pound fresh okra
8 cups fish broth
½ cup uncooked rice
1 teaspoon Worcestershire
   sauce
1 bunch parsley
1 pound crabmeat
¼ teaspoon salt
¼ teaspoon white pepper

1. Chop the onion and green pepper; sauté in butter in a pan over medium heat until the onion is soft.

2. Cube the tomatoes. Cut the okra into 1-inch pieces.

3. Combine the onion and green pepper with the tomatoes, okra, fish broth, rice, and Worcestershire sauce in the slow cooker.

4. Cover and heat on a low setting for 3 to 4 hours.

5. Chop the parsley and shred the crabmeat. Half an hour before serving, add the parsley, crab, salt, and pepper.

Festival Jambalaya

Serve this spicy dish with crusty French bread and beer.
And don't forget the zydeco music!

Serves 8–10

Cooking time: 4–5 hours
Preparation time: 60 minutes
Attention: Minimal
Pot size: 3–5 quarts

4 slices bacon
1 onion
3 cloves garlic
2 green peppers
1 cup uncooked rice
1 pound tomatoes
1 pound smoked ham
3½ cups chicken broth
1 pound shrimp
¼ teaspoon salt
½ teaspoon black pepper
¼ teaspoon red pepper sauce

1. Cut the bacon into 1-inch lengths. Dice the onion, crush and slice the garlic, and slice the green peppers.

2. Sauté the bacon in a pan over medium heat until transparent, then add the onion, garlic, and green peppers. Sauté until soft, then stir in the rice and heat for 5 minutes.

3. Chop the tomatoes and ham. Combine the rice mixture, tomatoes, ham, and broth in the slow cooker.

4. Cover and heat on a high setting for 1 hour, then on low for 3 to 4 hours.

5. Half an hour before serving, add the shrimp, salt, pepper, and red pepper sauce.

Beyond Chicken

If you have a hunter in the family, or a good butcher, you may have access to flavorful meats like pheasant, venison, or elk. Take advantage. Try a new meat in one of your standard recipes. Spaghetti with Elk Meatballs, anyone?

Sherry Jambalaya

Serves 10–12

Cooking time: 5–6 hours
Preparation time: 60 minutes
Attention: Minimal
Pot size: 3–5 quarts

3 onions
3 tablespoons butter
2 tomatoes
¼ teaspoon salt
½ teaspoon black pepper
1 bay leaf
2 cups uncooked brown rice
1½ pounds smoked ham
1 pound spicy pork sausage
1 tablespoon butter
4 cups chicken broth
1½ pounds mushrooms
1 pound shrimp, peeled and
    deveined
½ cup sherry
2 tablespoons butter

Every jambalaya is different—this one has sherry and lots of mushrooms.
Use wild mushrooms, like morels, if available.

1. Finely slice the onions; sauté in butter in a pan over medium heat until browned. Chop the tomatoes. Add the tomatoes, salt, pepper, bay leaf, and rice to the onions and continue to heat for 5 minutes.

2. Slice the ham. Brown the ham and sausage in butter. Drain; slice the sausage into bite-size pieces. Cut the ham into strips.

3. Combine the meat, rice mixture, and broth in the slow cooker.

4. Cover and heat on a high setting for 1 hour, then on low for 3 to 4 hours.

5. Slice the mushrooms. Braise the mushrooms and shrimp in the sherry and butter in a pan over medium heat. Half an hour before serving, pour the mushroom and shrimp mixture over the other ingredients. Do not stir.

Read All about It

Start a collection of antique cookbooks. In them you can find unique and fabulous menus and recipes. Look for these at used bookshops, rummage sales, swap meets, and library clearance sales. You might just find a new secret family recipe.

Roman Candle Short Ribs

As a variation, try using fresh jalapeno instead of pickled,
but use only a small spoonful to start.

Serves 10–12

Cooking time: 7–9 hours
Preparation time: 60 minutes
Attention: Minimal
Pot size: 3–5 quarts

5 pounds pork ribs
½ teaspoon white pepper
¼ teaspoon salt
2 tablespoons oil
¼ cup black olives
¼ teaspoon chili powder
4 cups barbecue sauce
1 bottle beer
¼ cup pickled jalapeno
*   peppers*

1. Cut the ribs into serving-size pieces. Boil the ribs in water with the white pepper and salt, then drain.

2. Sauté the ribs in oil in a pan over medium heat until browned.

3. Pit and slice the olives. Combine the ribs with the olives, chili powder, barbecue sauce, and beer in the slow cooker.

4. Cover and heat on a low setting for 6 to 8 hours.

5. Slice the jalapeno peppers. Half an hour before serving, stir in the jalapeno peppers.

Celebration Pudding

You can substitute other small dried fruits in this recipe.
Try dried cherries, or dried cranberries for a tart twist.

Yields 3 loaves

Cooking time: 2–3 hours
Preparation time: 45 minutes
Attention: Minimal
Pot size: 5 quarts

1 cup butter
1 cup sugar
8 eggs
2 cups milk
1 cup molasses
1 tablespoon baking powder
3 cups flour
2 lemons
¼ teaspoon mace
2 cups dried currants

1. Cream together the butter and sugar, then add the eggs, milk, and molasses. Sift the baking powder with the flour; add the flour mixture to the liquids.

2. Grate the lemon rinds. Stir the grated rind, mace, and currants into the batter.

3. Grease and flour 3 loaf pans or the equivalent. Fill the baking dishes one-half to three-quarters full; cover each dish with foil or a glass or ceramic lid. Arrange the dishes on a trivet or rack in the slow cooker, and pour water around the base of the trivet.

4. Cover and heat on a high setting for 2 to 3 hours.

Got Rhubarb?

Rhubarb, often considered a pest by anyone with a prolific patch in his yard, freezes beautifully. Harvest it often, chop it, and freeze it by the bagful. In the winter, pull it out and stew it with sweet fruit, liqueurs, and meats.

Independence Dinners

Start a revolution in your kitchen.
Let the guests, including kids, put together their own Independence Dinners,
which can cook while you watch fireworks.

Serves 8

Cooking time: 3–4 hours
Preparation time: 45 minutes
Attention: Minimal
Pot size: 3–5 quarts

1 onion
1 clove garlic
2 pounds hamburger
1 cup bread crumbs
1 tablespoon Worcestershire
   sauce
½ teaspoon salt
½ teaspoon black pepper
16 baby red potatoes
24 baby carrots
16 asparagus spears
2 yellow bell peppers
16 cherry tomatoes
½ teaspoon salt
½ teaspoon black pepper
Aluminum foil

1. Mince the onion and garlic. Combine with hamburger, crumbs, Worcestershire sauce, ½ teaspoon salt, and ½ teaspoon pepper and mix well. Divide the mixture into 8 patties or 16 balls.

2. Clean and halve the potatoes and carrots. Clean and trim the asparagus and yellow peppers; cut into 4-inch lengths.

3. Cut 8 1-foot lengths of heavy-duty aluminum foil (or double thickness of standard aluminum foil). In the center of each foil square, put one portion: 1 patty (or 2 balls) of meat mixture, 2 potatoes, 3 carrots, some asparagus, some pepper slices, and 2 cherry tomatoes. Sprinkle with salt and pepper and fold edges to seal.

4. Arrange on a trivet or rack in the slow cooker. Pour water around the base of the trivet.

5. Cover and heat on a high setting for 3 to 4 hours.

A Chemistry Trick

If your vegetables are giving off too much odor while you cook, simmer a small pan of vinegar on top of the stove at the same time, or immediately afterward. The vinegar fumes will help neutralize odors in the air.

Paul Revere Baked Beans

*A colonial classic—but now you don't have to keep
the woodstove burning all day to get the same tasty result.*

Serves 10–12

Cooking time: 8–10 hours
Preparation time: 30 minutes
Attention: Minimal
Pot size: 5 quarts

3 cups dried white beans
4 slices bacon
½ clove garlic
1 cup water
½ cup molasses
*1 tablespoon prepared
    mustard*
¼ teaspoon salt

1. Soak the beans overnight in cold water; drain.

2. Cut the bacon into 1-inch lengths. Crush and mince the garlic. Combine the bacon and garlic with soaked beans, 1 cup water, molasses, mustard, and salt in the slow cooker.

3. Cover and heat on a low setting for 8 to 10 hours.

Caramel Apples

*You would certainly eat an apple a day if you could prepare them like this.
For a fun twist, let your guests dip their own.*

Serves 8

Cooking time: 1–2 hours
Preparation time: 15 minutes
Attention: Minimal
Pot size: 3–5 quarts

2 pounds caramels
¼ cup water
8 apples

1. Unwrap the caramels and put them in the slow cooker with the water.

2. Cover and heat on a high setting for 1 to 2 hours. Stir periodically. Add more water to thin the caramel, if needed.

3. Skewer the apples on sticks and dip them into the melted caramel. Place apples on buttered waxed paper to cool.

Trick-or-Treat Caramel Corn

You can substitute roasted and salted peanuts, walnuts, or even macadamia nuts for pecans in this recipe. Better yet: use all of the above.

1. Melt ½ cup butter in a saucepan over low heat; add the sugar and syrup. Increase to medium heat and let simmer 6 minutes while stirring.

2. Remove the saucepan from the heat and add the cream of tartar, salt, and baking soda, stirring well.

3. Butter the inside of the slow cooker with the remaining 2 tablespoons butter. Put the popped corn in the slow cooker. Pour the liquid caramel over the top while mixing.

4. Cover and heat on a low setting for 1 to 2 hours. Stir periodically.

5. After the popcorn and caramel are mixed, add the pecans and mix again.

Serves 10–12

Cooking time: 1–2 hours
Preparation time: 45 minutes
Attention: Moderate
Pot size: 5 quarts

½ cup butter
1 cup brown sugar
¼ cup white corn syrup
⅛ teaspoon cream of tartar
½ teaspoon salt
½ teaspoon baking soda
2 tablespoons butter
3 quarts popped corn
1 cup roasted, salted pecans

Caramel Apple Bread Pudding

Set aside your favorite candies to be tucked into
this delicious dessert before it cooks.

Cooking time: 2–3 hours
Preparation time: 45 minutes
Attention: Minimal
Pot size: 3–5 quarts

2 tablespoons butter
3 cups cubed dry bread
½ cup caramels
1 apple
1 tablespoon butter
2 eggs
2 teaspoons vanilla
¾ cup sugar
¼ cup unsweetened cocoa
powder
½ teaspoon ground
cinnamon
2 cups milk

1. Butter 2 loaf pans or the equivalent. Distribute the bread cubes between the baking dishes, using enough bread to cover the bottom of each.

2. Cut the caramels into quarters. Peel, core, and dice the apple. Sprinkle the caramel and apple pieces over the bread. Melt the remaining butter and pour it over the bread pieces.

3. Beat the eggs. Add the vanilla, sugar, cocoa, cinnamon, and milk to the eggs. Pour the egg mixture carefully over the bread cubes to fill dishes one-half to three-quarters full.

4. Cover each dish with foil or a glass or ceramic lid. Arrange the dishes on a trivet or rack in the slow cooker, and pour water around the base of the trivet.

5. Cover and heat on a high setting for 2 to 3 hours.

Crouton Creativity

There are more places to use croutons than in salads. Make your own crouton variety pack. Broil pumpernickel cubes with garlic paste and butter, rye with crushed sage and olive oil, or sourdough with chili pepper and corn oil. Keep them in the freezer as a quick garnish for soups, stews, and other dishes, including salads.

Jack-o'-Lantern Bread

This bread freezes well. Make it ahead of your party, freeze, and then thaw and bring out the day guests arrive.

1. Sift the flour, baking soda, salt, and spices to mix.

2. Blend the sugar with the shortening, then blend in the eggs. Add the pumpkin and water to the egg mixture. Add the liquid mixture to the flour mixture and stir well. Fold in the raisins and nuts.

3. Grease and flour 2 loaf pans or the equivalent. Fill the baking dishes three-quarters or less full; cover each dish with foil or a glass or ceramic lid. Arrange the dishes on a trivet or rack in the slow cooker, and pour water around the base of the trivet.

4. Cover and heat on a high setting for 2 to 3 hours.

In a Hurry?

Yes, it would be nice to cook everything from scratch, but let's get real. Look closely at any recipe you choose. Can you substitute canned or frozen for something fresh? Can you pop in a couple of jars of salsa instead of onion, tomato, and chili?

Yields 2 loaves

Cooking time: 2–3 hours
Preparation time: 45 minutes
Attention: Minimal
Pot size: 3–5 quarts

3½ cups flour
2 teaspoons baking soda
1½ teaspoons salt
1 teaspoon cinnamon
1 teaspoon nutmeg
3 cups sugar
1 cup shortening
4 eggs
2 cups pumpkin
⅔ cup water
1 cup raisins
½ cup chopped nuts

Hot Cranberry Sauce

*Why buy that quivering canned cranberry sauce?
Make the real thing yourself. And add some orange rind for extra zing.*

Yields about 6 cups

Cooking time: 2–3 hours
Preparation time: 15 minutes
Attention: Minimal
Pot size: 3–5 quarts

*2 pounds fresh cranberries
4 cups sugar
½ cup water*

1. Mix the cranberries, sugar, and water in the slow cooker.

2. Cover and heat on a high setting for 2 to 3 hours.

Apricot Sweet Potatoes

*Try substituting dried peaches for apricots, or supplementing with dried
cherries. You can also use 2 tablespoons of molasses instead of the brown sugar.*

Serves 6–8

Cooking time: 5–6 hours
Preparation time: 30 minutes
Attention: Minimal
Pot size: 3–5 quarts

*1½ pounds sweet potatoes
1 pound dried apricots
⅓ cup raisins
1 tablespoon cornstarch
2 cups water
3 tablespoons brown sugar
¼ teaspoon salt
⅛ teaspoon cinnamon
3 tablespoons sherry
¼ orange*

1. Peel and slice the potatoes. Cut the apricots into quarters. Intermingle the potatoes, apricots, and raisins in the slow cooker.

2. Dissolve the cornstarch in ¼ cup of water in a mixing bowl, then add the remaining water, sugar, salt, cinnamon, and sherry. Grate the orange peel and add.

3. Add the liquid mixture to the slow cooker.

4. Cover and heat on a low setting for 5 to 6 hours.

Pilgrim Dressing

*Make your own version of this to use with
leftover turkey, ham, stuffing, or cranberries after the holidays.*

Serves 12–16

Cooking time: 4–5 hours
Preparation time: 45 minutes
Attention: Moderate
Pot size: 5 quarts

*1 pound mushrooms
1 clove garlic
2 cups sliced onion
2 cups sliced celery
¼ cup butter
12 cups dried bread cubes
2 teaspoons sage
1 teaspoon marjoram
½ cup white raisins
1 cup butter
2 eggs
4 cups poultry broth*

1. Slice the mushrooms. Crush and slice the garlic. Sauté the onion and celery in ¼ cup butter in a pan over low heat until the onion is soft, then add the mushrooms and garlic and continue heating another 10 minutes.

2. Mix the bread cubes and herbs in the slow cooker. Add the onion mixture and raisins. Mix well.

3. Melt the remaining butter and drizzle it over the bread cube mixture. Stir the eggs into the poultry broth, then pour the broth over the bread cube mixture while stirring.

4. Cover and heat on a high setting for 1 hour, then on low for 3 to 4 hours. Stir every hour.

Stuffing, Every Day

You don't need a turkey to have an excuse to make stuffing. Add combinations of apples, cranberries, mashed potatoes, dill pickles, chestnuts, oysters, chopped nuts, raisins, and wild rice to some seasoned bread cubes; dampen with some broth; and steam in your slow cooker. This is a great way to get rid of holiday leftovers.

Christmas Pudding

This is excellent served warm with lemon ice cream.
Use cake flour instead of all-purpose flour in this recipe.

Yields 2 loaves

Cooking time: 3–4 hours
Preparation time: 60 minutes
Attention: Minimal
Pot size: 3–5 quarts

2¼ cups flour
1 teaspoon baking soda
¼ teaspoon allspice
¼ teaspoon cinnamon
¼ teaspoon cloves
½ cup butter
1 cup sugar
4 eggs
½ cup rum
1½ cups raisins
½ cup sour cream

1. Sift the flour with the baking soda and spices to mix.

2. Cream the butter and sugar in a separate dish. Add the eggs to the creamed mixture and stir well. Warm the rum in a saucepan over low heat until steaming. Add the raisins to the saucepan and let them plump.

3. Blend the dry ingredients into the butter-and-sugar mixture gradually, alternating with the stewed raisin mixture and the sour cream.

4. Fill 2 greased and floured loaf pans, or the equivalent, one-half to three-quarters full with the batter. Loosely cover each dish with foil or other lid. Place on a trivet or rack in the slow cooker, and pour water around the base.

5. Cover and heat on a high setting for 3 to 4 hours.

California Desert Christmas Cake

This citrus-free fruitcake may be all you want for Christmas.
Try substituting dried cherries stewed in brandy or rum for glazed ones.

Yields 1 loaf

Cooking time: 2–3 hours
Preparation time: 30 minutes
Attention: Minimal
Pot size: 3–5 quarts

1 pound pitted dates
½ pound pitted glazed
    cherries
1 pound walnuts
1 cup flour
1 teaspoon baking powder
½ teaspoon salt
4 eggs
1 cup sugar
1 teaspoon vanilla

1. Put the fruit and nuts, uncut, in a mixing bowl.

2. Sift together the flour, baking powder, and salt to mix; add to fruit mix. Mix with hands to avoid damaging fruit.

3. Separate the eggs. Set aside the whites. Beat the yolks, then add the sugar and vanilla. Add to the flour and fruit mixture. Beat the whites until stiff. Add to the other ingredients and mix well, but carefully.

4. Grease and flour 1 loaf pan or the equivalent. Fill the baking dish one-half to three-quarters full; cover the dish with foil or a glass or ceramic lid. Arrange the dish on a trivet or rack in the slow cooker, and pour water around the base of the trivet.

5. Cover and heat on a high setting for 2 to 3 hours.

Keep a Lid on It

If you don't have glass lids for your baking pans or custard cups, use a double thickness of clean paper made waterproof by rubbing with butter or oil. The lid is mainly to keep out condensation, so it doesn't need to be as sturdy as glass.

Midnight Star Christmas Cake

*Try this toasted with honey butter. You can also soak this
with some extra brandy after cooking, for extra rich flavor.*

Yields 3 loaves

Cooking time: 2–3 hours
Preparation time: 60 minutes
Attention: Minimal
Pot size: 3–5 quarts

1 cup flour
½ teaspoon ground cloves
½ teaspoon ground ginger
½ tablespoon allspice
½ teaspoon cinnamon
1 orange
1 lemon
1 cup citron
3 cups currants
2 cups raisins
1 cup dried cherries
1 cup butter
1 cup sugar
5 eggs
¼ cup molasses
½ cup brandy

1. Sift the flour; blend with the spices. Grate the orange and lemon peels; mince the citron. Add the grated peels, citron, currants, raisins, and cherries to the dry ingredients.

2. Cut the butter into the sugar; stir in the eggs, molasses, and brandy. Squeeze the juice from the remaining (grated) lemon and add to the liquid mixture.

3. Combine the liquid and dry mixtures.

4. Grease and flour 3 loaf pans or the equivalent. Fill the baking dishes one-half to three-quarters full; cover each dish with foil or a glass or ceramic lid. Arrange the dishes on a trivet or rack in the slow cooker, and pour water around the base of the trivet.

5. Cover and heat on a high setting for 2 to 3 hours.

Smoother Baked Apples
Before baking apples, make several cuts down the sides. This will keep the skin from shriveling. Steaming them instead of baking also helps reduce the wrinkling.

Prairie Corn Pudding

This steaming corn dish is delicious in the morning with real maple syrup.
Serve a few sizzling sausages on the side.

1. Scald 1 cup of milk in a saucepan over medium heat, stirring constantly. Add the cornmeal and simmer over low heat for 20 minutes.

2. Mix the molasses, ginger, salt, and butter. Add to the cornmeal mixture.

3. Pour into a baking dish, filling one-half to three-quarters full. Pour ½ cup of milk over top. Cover the dish with foil or a glass or ceramic lid and arrange on a trivet or rack in the slow cooker. Pour water around the base of the trivet.

4. Cover and heat on a high setting for 1 to 2 hours.

Serves 4

Cooking time: 2–3 hours
Preparation time: 30 minutes
Attention: Minimal
Pot size: 3–5 quarts

1 cup milk
5 tablespoons cornmeal
⅔ cup molasses
1 teaspoon ground ginger
½ teaspoon salt
2 tablespoons butter
½ cup milk

Sweet Potatoes and Apples

Try this recipe with your favorite baking apple.
This dish is delicious as a side with ham or turkey.

1. Peel the potatoes and the apples. Thinly slice the potatoes; core and slice the apples. Mix the sugar, salt, and mace together.

2. Use half of the butter to grease the slow cooker, then assemble layers: potatoes (at the bottom), apples, brown sugar mixture, dabs of butter. Repeat.

3. Cover and heat on a low setting for 4 to 5 hours.

Serves 12

Cooking time: 4–5 hours
Preparation time: 30 minutes
Attention: Minimal
Pot size: 3–5 quarts

6 sweet potatoes
2 apples
½ cup brown sugar
½ teaspoon salt
1 teaspoon mace
½ cup butter

appendix A:
manufacturers of slow cookers and accessories

Slow Cookers

- All-Clad
- Cuisinart
- Delonghi
- Farberware
- Hamilton Beach
- Kenmore
- Morphy Richards
- Nesco
- Prima
- Proctor Silex
- Rival
- Russell Hobbs
- Swan
- Tefal
- Ultrex
- West Bend
- Zojirushi

Accessories

pans

- Rival Bread 'N' Cake Bake Pans

insulated traveling cases

- Rival
- West Bend

timers

- Rival Smart Part

appendix B:
flavors of liqueurs to use in slow cooking

- **Anise:** anisette, ouzo, or Sambuca
- **Apple:** Calvados
- **Black raspberry:** Chambord
- **Cherry:** kirsch or kirschwasser
- **Chocolate:** crème de cacao
- **Citrus:** Cointreau, curaçao, Gran Marnier, or Triple Sec
- **Coffee:** Kahlua or Tia Maria
- **Honey:** Chartreuse or Drambuie
- **Nuts:** Amaretto (almond), Frangelico or Noisette (hazelnut)
- **Pear:** Poire Williams
- **Plum:** slivovitz, Mirabelle, or Quetsch

Index

P

W

THE EVERYTHING SERIES!

BUSINESS & PERSONAL FINANCE

Everything® Budgeting Book
Everything® Business Planning Book
Everything® Coaching and Mentoring Book
Everything® Fundraising Book
Everything® Get Out of Debt Book
Everything® Grant Writing Book
Everything® Home-Based Business Book
Everything® Homebuying Book, 2nd Ed.
Everything® Homeselling Book, 2nd Ed.
Everything® Investing Book, 2nd Ed.
Everything® Landlording Book
Everything® Leadership Book
Everything® Managing People Book
Everything® Negotiating Book
Everything® Online Business Book
Everything® Personal Finance Book
Everything® Personal Finance in Your 20s
    and 30s Book
Everything® Project Management Book
Everything® Real Estate Investing Book
Everything® Robert's Rules Book, $7.95
Everything® Selling Book
Everything® Start Your Own Business Book
Everything® Wills & Estate Planning Book

COOKING

Everything® Barbecue Cookbook
Everything® Bartender's Book, $9.95
Everything® Chinese Cookbook
Everything® Cocktail Parties and Drinks
    Book
Everything® College Cookbook
Everything® Cookbook
Everything® Cooking for Two Cookbook
Everything® Diabetes Cookbook
Everything® Easy Gourmet Cookbook
Everything® Fondue Cookbook
Everything® Gluten-Free Cookbook

Everything® Grilling Cookbook
Everything® Healthy Meals in Minutes
    Cookbook
Everything® Holiday Cookbook
Everything® Indian Cookbook
Everything® Italian Cookbook
Everything® Low-Carb Cookbook
Everything® Low-Fat High-Flavor Cookbook
Everything® Low-Salt Cookbook
Everything® Meals for a Month Cookbook
Everything® Mediterranean Cookbook
Everything® Mexican Cookbook
Everything® One-Pot Cookbook
Everything® Pasta Cookbook
Everything® Quick Meals Cookbook
Everything® Slow Cooker Cookbook
Everything® Slow Cooking for a Crowd
    Cookbook
Everything® Soup Cookbook
Everything® Thai Cookbook
Everything® Vegetarian Cookbook
Everything® Wine Book, 2nd Ed.

CRAFT SERIES

Everything® Crafts—Baby Scrapbooking
Everything® Crafts—Bead Your Own Jewelry
Everything® Crafts—Create Your Own
    Greeting Cards
Everything® Crafts—Easy Projects
Everything® Crafts—Polymer Clay for
    Beginners
Everything® Crafts—Rubber Stamping
    Made Easy
Everything® Crafts—Wedding Decorations
    and Keepsakes

HEALTH

Everything® Alzheimer's Book
Everything® Diabetes Book
Everything® Health Guide to Controlling
    Anxiety

Everything® Hypnosis Book
Everything® Low Cholesterol Book
Everything® Massage Book
Everything® Menopause Book
Everything® Nutrition Book
Everything® Reflexology Book
Everything® Stress Management Book

HISTORY

Everything® American Government Book
Everything® American History Book
Everything® Civil War Book
Everything® Irish History & Heritage Book
Everything® Middle East Book

HOBBIES & GAMES

Everything® Blackjack Strategy Book
Everything® Brain Strain Book, $9.95
Everything® Bridge Book
Everything® Candlemaking Book
Everything® Card Games Book
Everything® Card Tricks Book, $9.95
Everything® Cartooning Book
Everything® Casino Gambling Book, 2nd Ed.
Everything® Chess Basics Book
Everything® Craps Strategy Book
Everything® Crossword and Puzzle Book
Everything® Crossword Challenge Book
Everything® Cryptograms Book, $9.95
Everything® Digital Photography Book
Everything® Drawing Book
Everything® Easy Crosswords Book
Everything® Family Tree Book, 2nd Ed.
Everything® Games Book, 2nd Ed.
Everything® Knitting Book
Everything® Knots Book
Everything® Photography Book
Everything® Poker Strategy Book
Everything® Pool & Billiards Book
Everything® Quilting Book
Everything® Scrapbooking Book

All Everything® books are priced at $12.95 or $14.95, unless otherwise stated. Prices subject to change without notice.

Everything® Sewing Book
Everything® Test Your IQ Book, $9.95
Everything® Travel Crosswords Book, $9.95
Everything® Woodworking Book
Everything® Word Games Challenge Book
Everything® Word Search Book

HOME IMPROVEMENT

Everything® Feng Shui Book
Everything® Feng Shui Decluttering Book,
    $9.95
Everything® Fix-It Book
Everything® Homebuilding Book
Everything® Lawn Care Book
Everything® Organize Your Home Book

EVERYTHING® *KIDS'* BOOKS

All titles are $6.95
Everything® Kids' Animal Puzzle & Activity
    Book
Everything® Kids' Baseball Book, 3rd Ed.
Everything® Kids' Bible Trivia Book
Everything® Kids' Bugs Book
Everything® Kids' Christmas Puzzle
    & Activity Book
Everything® Kids' Cookbook
Everything® Kids' Crazy Puzzles Book
Everything® Kids' Dinosaurs Book
Everything® Kids' Gross Jokes Book
Everything® Kids' Gross Puzzle and
    Activity Book
Everything® Kids' Halloween Puzzle
    & Activity Book
Everything® Kids' Hidden Pictures Book
Everything® Kids' Joke Book
Everything® Kids' Knock Knock Book
Everything® Kids' Math Puzzles Book
Everything® Kids' Mazes Book
Everything® Kids' Money Book
Everything® Kids' Nature Book
Everything® Kids' Puzzle Book
Everything® Kids' Riddles & Brain Teasers Book
Everything® Kids' Science Experiments Book
Everything® Kids' Sharks Book
Everything® Kids' Soccer Book
Everything® Kids' Travel Activity Book

KIDS' STORY BOOKS

Everything® Fairy Tales Book

LANGUAGE

Everything® Conversational Japanese Book
    (with CD), $19.95
Everything® French Phrase Book, $9.95
Everything® French Verb Book, $9.95
Everything® Inglés Book
Everything® Learning French Book
Everything® Learning German Book
Everything® Learning Italian Book
Everything® Learning Latin Book
Everything® Learning Spanish Book
Everything® Sign Language Book
Everything® Spanish Grammar Book
Everything® Spanish Practice Book
    (with CD), $19.95
Everything® Spanish Phrase Book, $9.95
Everything® Spanish Verb Book, $9.95

MUSIC

Everything® Drums Book (with CD), $19.95
Everything® Guitar Book
Everything® Home Recording Book
Everything® Playing Piano and Keyboards
    Book
Everything® Reading Music Book (with CD),
    $19.95
Everything® Rock & Blues Guitar Book
    (with CD), $19.95
Everything® Songwriting Book

NEW AGE

Everything® Astrology Book, 2nd Ed.
Everything® Dreams Book, 2nd Ed.
Everything® Ghost Book
Everything® Love Signs Book, $9.95
Everything® Numerology Book
Everything® Paganism Book
Everything® Palmistry Book
Everything® Psychic Book
Everything® Reiki Book
Everything® Tarot Book
Everything® Wicca and Witchcraft Book

PARENTING

Everything® Baby Names Book
Everything® Baby Shower Book
Everything® Baby's First Food Book
Everything® Baby's First Year Book
Everything® Birthing Book
Everything® Breastfeeding Book
Everything® Father-to-Be Book
Everything® Father's First Year Book
Everything® Get Ready for Baby Book
Everything® Get Your Baby to Sleep Book,
    $9.95
Everything® Getting Pregnant Book
Everything® Homeschooling Book
Everything® Mother's First Year Book
Everything® Parent's Guide to Children
    and Divorce
Everything® Parent's Guide to Children
    with ADD/ADHD
Everything® Parent's Guide to Children
    with Asperger's Syndrome
Everything® Parent's Guide to Children
    with Autism
Everything® Parent's Guide to Children with
    Bipolar Disorder
Everything® Parent's Guide to Children
    with Dyslexia
Everything® Parent's Guide to Positive
    Discipline
Everything® Parent's Guide to Raising a
    Successful Child
Everything® Parent's Guide to Tantrums
Everything® Parent's Guide to the Overweight
    Child
Everything® Parent's Guide to the Strong-
    Willed Child
Everything® Parenting a Teenager Book
Everything® Potty Training Book, $9.95
Everything® Pregnancy Book, 2nd Ed.
Everything® Pregnancy Fitness Book
Everything® Pregnancy Nutrition Book
Everything® Pregnancy Organizer, $15.00
Everything® Toddler Book
Everything® Tween Book
Everything® Twins, Triplets, and More Book

All Everything® books are priced at $12.95 or $14.95, unless otherwise stated. Prices subject to change without notice.

PETS

Everything® Cat Book
Everything® Dachshund Book
Everything® Dog Book
Everything® Dog Health Book
Everything® Dog Training and Tricks Book
Everything® German Shepherd Book
Everything® Golden Retriever Book
Everything® Horse Book
Everything® Horseback Riding Book
Everything® Labrador Retriever Book
Everything® Poodle Book
Everything® Pug Book
Everything® Puppy Book
Everything® Rottweiler Book
Everything® Small Dogs Book
Everything® Tropical Fish Book
Everything® Yorkshire Terrier Book

REFERENCE

Everything® Car Care Book
Everything® Classical Mythology Book
Everything® Computer Book
Everything® Divorce Book
Everything® Einstein Book
Everything® Etiquette Book, 2nd Ed.
Everything® Inventions and Patents Book
Everything® Mafia Book
Everything® Philosophy Book
Everything® Psychology Book
Everything® Shakespeare Book

RELIGION

Everything® Angels Book
Everything® Bible Book
Everything® Buddhism Book
Everything® Catholicism Book
Everything® Christianity Book
Everything® Jewish History & Heritage Book
Everything® Judaism Book
Everything® Koran Book
Everything® Prayer Book
Everything® Saints Book

Everything® Torah Book
Everything® Understanding Islam Book
Everything® World's Religions Book
Everything® Zen Book

SCHOOL & CAREERS

Everything® Alternative Careers Book
Everything® College Survival Book, 2nd Ed.
Everything® Cover Letter Book, 2nd Ed.
Everything® Get-a-Job Book
Everything® Guide to Starting and Running
    a Restaurant
Everything® Job Interview Book
Everything® New Teacher Book
Everything® Online Job Search Book
Everything® Paying for College Book
Everything® Practice Interview Book
Everything® Resume Book, 2nd Ed.
Everything® Study Book

SELF-HELP

Everything® Dating Book, 2nd Ed.
Everything® Great Sex Book
Everything® Kama Sutra Book
Everything® Self-Esteem Book

SPORTS & FITNESS

Everything® Fishing Book
Everything® Golf Instruction Book
Everything® Pilates Book
Everything® Running Book
Everything® Total Fitness Book
Everything® Weight Training Book
Everything® Yoga Book

TRAVEL

Everything® Family Guide to Hawaii
Everything® Family Guide to Las Vegas,
    2nd Ed.
Everything® Family Guide to New York City,
    2nd Ed.
Everything® Family Guide to RV Travel &
    Campgrounds

Everything® Family Guide to the Walt Disney
    World Resort®, Universal Studios®,
    and Greater Orlando, 4th Ed.
Everything® Family Guide to Cruise Vacations
Everything® Family Guide to the Caribbean
Everything® Family Guide to Washington
    D.C., 2nd Ed.
Everything® Guide to New England
Everything® Travel Guide to the Disneyland
    Resort®, California Adventure®,
    Universal Studios®, and the
    Anaheim Area

WEDDINGS

Everything® Bachelorette Party Book, $9.95
Everything® Bridesmaid Book, $9.95
Everything® Elopement Book, $9.95
Everything® Father of the Bride Book, $9.95
Everything® Groom Book, $9.95
Everything® Mother of the Bride Book, $9.95
Everything® Outdoor Wedding Book
Everything® Wedding Book, 3rd Ed.
Everything® Wedding Checklist, $9.95
Everything® Wedding Etiquette Book, $9.95
Everything® Wedding Organizer, $15.00
Everything® Wedding Shower Book, $9.95
Everything® Wedding Vows Book, $9.95
Everything® Weddings on a Budget Book,
    $9.95

WRITING

Everything® Creative Writing Book
Everything® Get Published Book
Everything® Grammar and Style Book
Everything® Guide to Writing a Book Proposal
Everything® Guide to Writing a Novel
Everything® Guide to Writing Children's Books
Everything® Guide to Writing Research Papers
Everything® Screenwriting Book
Everything® Writing Poetry Book
Everything® Writing Well Book

Available wherever books are sold!
To order, call 800-258-0929, or visit us at *www.everything.com*
Everything® and everything.com® are registered trademarks of F+W Publications, Inc.